A FLOWER-LOVER'S
MISCELLANY

* * *

PRINTED IN GREAT BRITAIN

PRINTED BY BILLING & SONS LTD,
GUILDFORD AND LONDON
112.561

PLATE I   Fuchsia, Azalea and Clematis   *(frontispiece*

(facing p. 3

A Flower-Lover's Miscellany

*An authoritative collection
of factual information
together with an account
of historical and
legendary associations*

by Daphne Barraclough

Illustrated by Esmé Eve

Frederick Warne & Co. Ltd, London and New York

FLOWERS

On the third day of creation,
Before mankind had birth,
Ten thousand thousand flowers sprang up
To beautify the earth.

And now and then ten thousand flowers
From the gracious earth outburst;
And every flower that springeth up
Is goodly as the first.

Empires have fallen to decay,
Forgotten e'en in name,
And Man's sublimest words decay;
But ye are still the same.

Ye flowers! – Ye little flowers
Were witnesses of things
More glorious and more wondrous far
Than the rise and fall of kings!

ANON

Contents

✳ ✳

Chapter		
	List of Plates	6
1	Flowers—The Unbroken Link	7
2	Legends, Superstitions and Folklore	18
3	The Rose of England	34
4	The Language of Flowers	39
5	Bottled Fragrance	46
6	Flower Wines	54
7	Flower Cookery	62
8	Flowers in Cosmetics	74
9	Pot-Pourri	79
10	Pollination and Seed Dispersal	86
11	Sports and Rarities	90
12	Preserving Flowers	98
13	A Handful of Flowers	102
14	Making Flower Pictures	119
15	Green Fingers	122
	Kill or Cure	140
16	The Herb Garden	142
17	Gardener's Corner	150
	Calendar of Floral Decoration	155

List of Illustrations

❋ ❋

Plate

I   Fuchsia, Azalea and Clematis   *Frontispiece*

Facing page

II, III   Flowers of Legend and Superstition 14 and 15

IV   Roses   48

V   Fragrant Flowers   64

VI   Flowers for Cookery   65

VII   Methods of Pollination and Seed Dispersal   96

VIII   August Selection   97

IX   Sports and Rarities   112

X   Flowers for Hanging Baskets and Wall Pots   128

XI   Climbing Plants   129

XII   Indoor Plants   144

CHAPTER I

Flowers

The Unbroken Link

Have you ever watched a poppy burst its bud and shake out its silken petals to the sun? And gazing into its dusky heart, have you seen only the wonder of nature at work, or have you perhaps glimpsed a fleeting vision of the mysterious East from whence it came?

To the flower-lover it is perhaps enough that the heart and eyes should be gladdened by the small miracle of the unfolding bud, and yet how much greater is our wealth when we pause to realize that within a simple bunch of flowers lies much of the history of the world.

The most exotic flower in our garden today is a descendant of the first vegetation which sprang from the earth for the service of man. Down the ages plants and flowers have been to man meat, drink and medicine. Every great occasion in life is graced by their beauty, expressing what the human language fails to do. The seasons are marked by them; the Victorians used them to evolve a flower language, and they still provide the sweetest perfumes and the most potent medicines.

The humblest flower of the hedgerow, no less than the cultivated hothouse bloom, holds within its petals a story to rank among the most wonderful the world has ever known. Long and fascinating is the history of every flower we know today, strange and romantic its passage across the world.

The fact which so many of us fail to grasp is that the flowers which grace our gardens are there only because of a deep-seated mixture of sentiment and superstition within the human race. Lost in admiration for a show of hyacinths or narcissus we are apt to forget that thousands of years ago these flowers were cultivated, not for the beauty of their petals, but for the bulbs which were an important item in the human diet. It has been estimated that 20,000 years or more ago the hyacinth and the onion shared the same plot of earth, being cultivated along with many other plants solely for the purpose of man's sustenance. The gay dahlia meant nothing more in those days than that its tubers provided valuable starchy food.

Why some plants are still used as food while others, though equally valuable sources of nourishment, are ignored is a difficult question to answer. The East Indian lotus finds great favour in the diet of Asiatic races today, and the fruit of the wild rose (rose hips), which was eaten in medieval times, is even today regarded as one of the finest sources of Vitamin C. On the other hand, while the medieval housewife appreciated the food value of violets and primroses, we are inclined to pass over these vitamin-rich salad foods in favour of less nutritious items.

The same question applies to medicine. Centuries ago plants were the one and only source of medicine, and the Bible tells us that the leaves of the trees are for the healing of the nations, and plants for the service of man. The modern herbalist claims that plants still provide the finest medicines, and certainly many common flowers are even today regarded as the source of some of the most potent drugs, while the pretty pyrethrum now provides us with a lethal insecticide.

❀   ❀   ❀

Advancement of time has wrought great changes, but reflecting on early civilization we get a glimpse of man deriving his meat and medicine from the profusion of plants that ran wild through forest and plain. His common sense undoubtedly led him to cultivate the earth close to his living quarters and there husband the plants which he used day by day.

New elements crept in as civilization advanced. The cultivation of grain to displace the dahlia as a starchy food was but one instance of the change in man's relation to plants. Perhaps when he no longer required the plants to sustain his body he had the opportunity to appreciate their beauty of blossom, or perhaps, perverse creature that he was, he valued them most when he needed them least. In either case sentiment undoubtedly played a part in the continued husbanding of flowers.

Apart from sentiment, superstition must have laid a strong hand on the course of events. The great impression made by the apparently mysterious blooming of certain flowers during certain seasons led to a series of religious ceremonies which even today are perpetuated in the form of our various flower festivals.

The regular blooming of certain flowers also led to the birth of the first floral calendar in countries where the climate ensured a continuous succession of blooms. At one time the Japanese year opened with the first plum blossom and closed with the fading of the camellias.

Thus, through sentiment, superstition, and no doubt an ever-growing love of the beauty of flowers, their cultivation turned from a task of necessity to a labour of love.

❋   ❋   ❋

Tracing back through the history of any flower we see about us today reveals an enthralling story of wonder and romance.

Many centuries ago plants started their wanderings across the world via the ancient trade routes. Similarity of soil and climate enabled peoples of different races to cultivate plants from other lands, but it is almost impossible to say which race pioneered their cultivation solely for the purpose of ornamentation.

From a labyrinth of information gleaned from ancient writings and primitive drawings the serious botanist gets glimpses of flower cultivation many centuries B.C. But to the ordinary flower-lover the later centuries invariably prove more fascinating.

When Marco Polo visited China between 1272 and 1293 it was obvious that the Chinese had already been practising ornamental cultivation for some centuries. The Chinese are an ancient race and have an inborn love of flowers and gardens, and it is to their country that we are indebted for some of our own garden favourites. Hollyhocks, almost inseparable from the English cottage garden, raised their giant stems in ancient China, and that country's mountains were long ago garlanded with peonies and regal lilies. Gay forsythia bringing cheer to bare gardens, clematis festooning the porch, and shaggy chrysanthemums heralding the approach of autumn whisper intriguing stories of the China of old.

It is to the Turks that we owe gratitude for the tulip, for it was they who first hybridized the best varieties. Asian countries had long known the tulip as a flower growing wild during the short spring, and it found its way into the hearts of the people to be cultivated as a garden flower. The Turks, however, went one better, hybridizing and selecting, and the very name tulip, meaning turban, will always serve to remind us of the early beginnings of one of our favourite spring flowers.

Well known for their love of flowers, the Japanese will spend hours over the arrangement of one or two blooms, showing a patience which could only have been inherited from their forbears. The exquisite flowers which have come to us from their country are a monument to the loving patience of the gardeners of a bygone age.

Perhaps it is not surprising that flowers which were grown and selected there should appear to us symbolic of the image which springs to mind whenever we think of Old Japan: the exquisite colouring, and the almost ethereal delicacy of form. What could one associate more with that ancient race than wisteria blossom tumbling gracefully over the veranda, its flowing lines and gentle tints extraordinarily reminiscent of kimonos and geisha girls?

It is to the everlasting credit of the ancient gardeners of Japan that they propagated and selected plants from other lands which otherwise might never have found their way into our gardens today, among them the flowering almond and peach from China. The Japanese azalea, too, was produced by crossing a Chinese strain with varieties native to Japan.

How many of us have not at some time or other pushed a few nasturtium seeds into the garden and marvelled at the riot of colour later produced. The profusion of flowers scrambling over one another in their eagerness to flaunt their gay petals should give us a clue to their native haunt, even if their characteristic smell does not at once bring to mind the prolific jungle.

Over fifty wild varieties of nasturtium flourish in the tropical regions between Chile and southern Mexico. The temperatures of these regions – contrary to popular belief – rarely exceed those of one of our heat-wave summers (admittedly somewhat rare), which perhaps explains why many flowers from the South American tropics have made their homes so happily in British gardens.

That the ancient Mexican races rivalled the Chinese in floral cultivation is an undoubted fact, and these remarkable flower-lovers hybridized the dahlia so long ago that it is almost impossible to trace the line of our present garden species to its original progenitors. Plant explorers have been astonished by the natural flair possessed by Mexican gardeners and the dexterity with which they cultivate their plants. This, coupled with the almost fanatical care they lavish upon the humblest flower, can only point to a deeply inherited love and knowledge of plants. The floral extravagance with which the poorest Mexican surrounds himself is sufficient to endear him for ever to flower-lovers everywhere.

South America in general has given us many of today's most popular garden flowers, her contribution owing its wide variety almost entirely to the diversity of her climate. Snow-capped mountains, humid jungle, exceptionally wet and intensely dry areas all combine to offer some plant suitable for cultivation in almost every other corner of the world; and fuchsias, salvias and petunias are only three of those with which the British flower-lover has sought to adorn his garden, whether it be country estate, suburban plot or town window-box.

Australia too has a fascinating little niche in the story of flowers. Botanists believe that countless centuries ago Australia was connected by land to New Zealand and Africa, but after she became separated by sea she evolved plants of a very individual type. Captain Cook's discovery of Australia opened up the first route by which many of these plants could make their escape to start their own voyage round the world. Notable among the wanderers is the helichrysum, or everlasting flower as we prefer to call it, whose great popularity is achieved no doubt by the unusual texture of its petals and the fact that if carefully dried after cutting it will provide indoor decoration at a period of the year when cut flowers are scarce and expensive.

Man has wrought wonders in the evolution of plants, but nothing achieved by the human hand can compare with the achievements of nature. The remarkable feat of the delicate little snowdrop, valiantly blooming against apparently over-whelming odds, ranks among the greatest wonders in the story of flowers, and is a classic example of nature at work adapting and contriving to take care of her own.

Thousands of years before the earliest civilization, these little flowers, together with other spring bloomers, are believed to have been inhabitants of warmer climes. The march of time imposed climatic changes which forced these plants to perform some adaptations in their method of propagation. To offset unfavourable conditions and the possibility of a short blooming period, a bulbous storage system was evolved whereby each plant preformed its next season's flowers immediately after its present season's blooming. Now, while the snowdrop and her fellow bulbous spring flowers are lying dormant in our woods and gardens, there are in fact, tucked safely away in the heart of each bulb, perfectly formed flowers and leaves quietly awaiting that mysterious call which heralds the approach of spring.

❊   ❊   ❊

Considering the pleasure man found in the ornamental cultivation of flowers it is not surprising that he should seek to extend his joy.

When the Romans made cultural contact with the Egyptians they were impressed by the flower paintings with which the interior walls of buildings were decorated. The Romans lost no time in taking up and developing this idea, and that they became highly skilled in their art is evident from the fine examples discovered during excavations at Pompeii.

Merchants and travellers carried reports of this new form of decoration until flower murals were appearing in many lands. Progress of time and the introduction of new materials and processes eventually led to the flower-printed wallpapers we know today, and though many centuries lie between these and the original wall paintings, the link that binds them is the flower motif.

The Persians made a special contribution to the evolution of this form of decoration. Faced with the necessity of bringing warmth to their homes during the cold winter months, they devised the idea of weaving their flower designs into tapestries and rugs. A flower-loving race who tended their plants with care, they based their designs upon

Honeysuckle

Columbine

Tulip

PLATE II   Flowers of Legend and Superstition

(facing p. 14

Ragged robin

Broom

St. John's wort

PLATE III   Flowers of Legend and Superstition

(facing p. 15

the formal layout of the Persian garden, and the weaving was so exquisitely done that in original examples still in existence it is possible to distinguish individual plant species. Present-day mechanically woven Persian carpets are still based on the original designs, though over the years the flowers have become stylized and can no longer be individually recognized.

❊   ❊   ❊

Thoughts relating to flowers invariably lead to the question of how each acquired the name by which we know it today.

The explanations are many and varied, but the most straightforward answers are to be found among flowers which have been named in honour of people who either made some special contribution to the flower world or were personalities in their own right. Among these are the fuchsias, which were named after Leonhard Fuchs, the sixteenth-century botanist, and the bird of paradise (*Strelitzia reginae*), which honours the wife of George III, Queen Charlotte Sophia of the House of Mecklenburg-Strelitz.

The names of many of our popular flowers, however, are inextricably entangled with the history of the world. In early times when country conquered country it was inevitable that foreign words should be absorbed into the tongue of many races. Over the centuries transpositions and modifications have altered many words until they now bear little resemblance to the originals.

Our gilliflower is one example of this evolution. When the Romans conquered the Greeks they acquired the Greek word *kauophullon* which they applied to plants with leaves shaped like those of the stock family. During subsequent conquests the name was carried into other countries and subtly altered in spelling and pronunciation until it appeared in the early French language as 'giroflee'. By the time it had reached England the word had become 'gilofre', and then through a succession of English modifications became in turn 'gilofer', 'giloflor', 'giliflour', until the name finally emerged as the 'gilliflower' we know today.

All our flower names, however, are not so easily accounted for. Indeed, some set a riddle which only surmise can solve. Names which have no apparent history often bear a strong resemblance to old family names of other lands, and it is generally assumed that in bygone days when some family acquired and jealously guarded a new and previously unknown plant, it automatically acquired the family's name.

The Michaelmas daisy – a prevalent American weed until plant explorers carried it into Europe, where it at once achieved popularity as a garden plant – acquired its name simply because of the magnificent show it puts on during the period of St. Michael's Mass.

The connective element is apparent in many plant names, especially those which in days gone by were put to medicinal and household use. When a decoction of herbs was considered to be a cure for sentimental affairs of the heart, the wild pansy was always administered, and thereby acquired its name of heart's ease.

A less romantic but none the less colourful reminder of our heritage is the sweet scabious. At a period in our history when soap and water had no part in the daily toilette almost every garden had its plot of scabious. Any beauty these pretty flowers brought to the garden was quite accidental, their cultivation being entirely as a cure for the itch – referred to in the language of the period as 'the scabious'.

It is a remarkable fact that having kept their original

descriptive names with very little modification some flowers have at the same time acquired others equally suggestive of their appearance. The antirrhinum is one example, its name being derived from a Greek word meaning 'in the shape of a nose'. The now more popular name of snapdragon also describes to perfection the impression of the snapping jaws of a dragon when the flower is squeezed gently from the sides.

The romantic side of human nature clings closely to the myths and legends surrounding flowers and their names. Who is there among us who would care to disbelieve the enchanting stories of the forget-me-not (page 22), our lady's bedstraw (page 28), the moss rose (page 27) and the lily of the valley (page 26), and all the other legends that bring a special charm to the wonderful story of flowers?

Down through the ages flowers have been man's constant companions, bringing nourishment and medicine to his body and joy to his soul. If he but loves the flowers by the wayside the humblest tramp on the highway is a rich man indeed, for in the words of the hymn, 'Daisies are our silver, Buttercups our gold': a simple song of praise written for little children, but therein lies a special meaning for the flower-lover of any age.

❊   ❊   ❊

Daffodils
    That come before the swallow dares, and take
    The winds of March with beauty.

SHAKESPEARE

The Daisy scattered on each mead and down,
A golden tuft within a silver crown.

BROWNE'S PASTORALS

B

CHAPTER 2

Legends

Superstitions and Folklore

Deep in the heart of almost every human being there is a strong vein of superstition, and flowers have their share in this. Most of us know people who will not have lilac or bluebells or perhaps hawthorn blossom in their homes because they think it will bring bad luck. They are completely at a loss to explain how this happens and have no real excuse for their superstition except that perhaps their grandmother had told them it was so.

Old country names often give a clue to the folklore surrounding various flowers. Children in some districts know cow parsley by the name of mother die and will not pick it for fear of the consequences. The gathering of the pretty little blue bird's eye is reputed in other places to result in birds pecking out the eyes of the transgressor.

Flowers are surrounded by folklore and legend, and yet while a large number of gardening experts know all the answers concerning tongue-twisting Latin names, very few of them know the delightful legends attached to flowers from which many derived their ordinary names. The following selection covers some of our most popular and well-known flowers.

Adonis. This plant derives its name from the Greek legends concerning Adonis, from whose blood it is supposed to have sprung.

Agrimony. In olden days agrimony was considered to be protective against the bite of serpents.

Anemone. There are many delightful legends regarding the origin of the anemone. One of the most persistent is that Anemone was a nymph greatly beloved by Zephyr. Flora was so jealous of Anemone's beauty that she banished her from court, and finally transformed her into the flower.

Bachelor's Button. To test success of a love affair a bachelor's button should be carried in the pocket. If the flower keeps fresh so will the romance. If it quickly fades the romance can be expected to wither also.

Basil. It is said that the common basil will wither in the hands of the impure.

Belladonna. In Bohemia belladonna is supposed to be a favourite plant of the Devil. By letting loose a black hen on Walpurgis Night the Devil will be tempted to spring from the flower to chase the hen.

Bramble. For the bramble to bloom early in June is a sign of a good harvest.

Broom. Broom figures in many legends and superstitions, and also plays a part in history. The Plantagenet kings took their name from the broom (*Planta genista*), and according to legend Genfroi, Earl of Anjou, the father of Henry II, chose a sprig of broom to wear in his hat as he went into battle.

The collar of the order of Colle de Genet, formed by

St. Louis of France, consisted of broom flowers intermingled with fleur-de-lis.

Broom buds were eaten at the coronation banquet of King James II.

In China the leaves of the broom are salted and made into broom leaf tea.

Country folk say that if the broom is heavy with blossom the corn crops will also be heavy.

Candytuft. Because of its shape and construction the candytuft is regarded in France as the emblem of architecture.

This flower was introduced into England in the reign of Elizabeth I, and came from Candie in the island of Crete.

Clover. The Druids held the clover as a charm against evil spirits.

The fact that white clover often springs up in profusion when virgin moorland soil is turned over for the first time has led to the countryman's belief that where the white clover grows the soil is especially rich and productive.

Bohemian girls secretly place clover leaves in their lovers' shoes before they set out on a journey to ensure that they will remain true to them whilst they are away.

Coltsfoot. In Bavaria on Easter Day the peasants make garlands of this little flower and then cast them into the fire.

Columbine (Aquilegia). This pretty flower takes its name from the Latin *aquila* – the eagle – because of the resemblance of the flower's 'spurs' to an eagle's talons.

Cowslip. In Lancashire the cowslip is widely known as the fairy's cup.

Daffodil. Legend records that Prosperine was picking daffodils in Sicily when she was stolen away by Pluto.

Daisy (Bellis). According to legend the daisy derived its

name from the Belides, who transformed a beautiful dryad who was beloved by Ephigeus into a daisy flower to protect her from the attentions of Verlummus.

At the wedding reception of Charles the Bold of Burgundy and Princess Margaret of England the two nations were represented by a toy leopard which held in one claw the standard of England and in the other a daisy (the daisy being known in France as the marguerite).

Spring does not arrive in the North until you can put your foot on twelve daisies.

Dandelion. The dandelion is the centre of many legends and much folklore. In the country it is widely known as the shepherd's clock, owing to its habit of opening at 5 a.m. and closing again at 8 p.m.

An old superstition says that if you blow upon the seed head and one single aigrette remains the loved one is thinking of you.

If the aigrettes float away from the seed head when there is no wind it is a sign of rain.

It is generally supposed that the dandelion derived its name from the resemblance of its leaves to a lion's jaw and teeth (*dent-de-lion*).

Dock. In Cornwall the leaves of the dock are wetted with spring water and applied to burns.

In most parts of the country the leaves are used on nettle stings. The correct method is to hold the leaves to the affected part and repeat 'Out nettle, in dock; dock shall have a new smock'.

Elder. Legends and superstitions relating to the elder tree, its leaves and blossom are numerous and varied, and appear in many countries and among widely differing peoples.

In Scandinavian mythology the elder tree is dedicated to the Goddess of Love and Thor, the God of Thunder.

The Danes believe that a being known as the 'Elder Mother' lives in the tree, and that she will avenge any injury which is done to any part of it.

Many people will not have furniture made from the wood of the elder tree in their homes, believing it to bring ill luck.

It is said that anyone who stands in the shade of an elder tree at midnight will see the King of the Elves go by with his retinue.

In the Tyrol the peasants regard the tree so highly that they raise their hats when passing it.

An old country remedy for toothache is to suck a small twig of elder.

In some countries an elder stick is used during wedding ceremonies to bring luck to the bridal pair.

Many a Sussex countryman carries an elder stick with three or more notches cut into it to protect him from rheumatism.

It is widely supposed that the Cross was made from elder wood, and for this reason Gloucestershire people will not burn any part of the elder tree.

For the same reason it is said that lightning will never strike an elder tree.

Forget-me-not. Legend has a charming little story regarding the origin of the forget-me-not. Along the banks of the River Danube one day long ago a knight strolled with his beloved. Suddenly the maiden espied floating downstream a posy of dainty blue flowers, and was so enchanted with their beauty that she begged her knight to get them for her. True gallant that he was, he dived into the water for them. Hampered by his cumbersome armour he was unable to reach the bank again, but he threw the posy of flowers to the feet of the maiden, and as he sank below the surface for ever he called to her 'Forget me not'.

Foxglove. This delightful flower is closely associated with fairies and elves, and is considered to be their especial hiding place in woodland and gardens.

Digitalis, derived from a Latin word for finger, probably led to the name of fairies' gloves by which these flowers are widely known. The bad fairies are supposed to allow the fox to cover his paws with the flower bells to conceal his footprints.

The foxglove is of course a well-known source of medicine for heart complaints.

The fairy associations are extremely prevalent in Ireland, where the flower bells are considered to be used by the little folk as caps, petticoats and thimbles.

Globe Flower. Peasants in the Swiss Alps make garlands of globe flowers for use during local festivities.

In northern counties of Britain the flowers were once used to decorate cottage doors to herald the month of June.

Gorse. The old saying that 'Kissing is out of season when gorse is out of bloom' no doubt arose from the fact that it is rarely that the gorse can be found to be completely devoid of blossoms.

Harebell. One of the most delicate of flowers, the harebell has been assigned to St. George, as this little rhyme denotes:

> On St. George's Day when blue is worn,
> The blue harebells the fields adorn.

Hawthorn (May Blossom). According to ancient mythology

the hawthorn tree sprang from lightning, and it has been held sacred ever since.

The Greeks garland their brides with the blossoms and decorate the altars with them for the wedding ceremony. They suspend branches of flowering hawthorn over their doorways on May-day, and newlyweds are escorted to their rooms by torches of hawthorn wood.

In England the coming of the month of May was always celebrated in traditional form, flowering branches of hawthorn being hung over every door.

The custom of 'going a-maying' has died out in all but a few country districts, but in bygone days all the young people used to rise before dawn and go out into the woods and lanes from where they gathered the flowering branches. These they formed into garlands with which they adorned themselves and returned in procession at sunrise, carrying armfuls of hawthorn flowers to decorate their houses. The procession was accompanied by musicians, and merrymaking followed throughout the day. The crowning of a May Queen and May-day sports for children are almost the only connection with the old tradition of 'maying'.

King Henry VII was crowned with a crown formed from the hawthorn tree after King Richard III was killed in battle at Bosworth.

An old country belief is that when the hawthorn trees are heavy with blossom a bad winter will follow.

In Brittany and some parts of Ireland this tree is known as the fairy thorn, and is thought to be the trysting place of the fairy folk.

Heather. The Scots hold this attractive plant in great esteem, and use it in many ways. Many old crofters living in the wilder parts of the country sleep on beds of heather which are extremely comfortable and springy. Ropes are fashioned from the fibres, and a very strong orange dye is obtained from the plant.

Another use for heather blossom is as a drink flavouring, and the honey produced from the activity of the bees among the purple carpet is considered by many people to be the finest of all honeys.

Honesty. It is said that where purple honesty thrives, the gardener who tends it is exceptionally honest himself.

Honeysuckle. In bygone times this flower was thought to possess great powers, and if a person fell ill a circular wreath was made from the plant through which the patient was passed three times.

Jasmine. Jasmine flowers form a large proportion of the bases of many modern perfumes, and yet the world might never have had the pleasure of enjoying this sweetly per-fumed flower had it not been for the act of a Tuscan gardener.

The gardener to the Grand Duke of Tuscany was so badly paid that he was unable to marry the maiden of his choice. Then one day in 1699 the duke obtained a very rare specimen of jasmine and refused to allow it to be propagated. The gardener, however, managed to carry a tiny sprig of it to his betrothed on her birthday and instructed her in the details of its cultivation. The sprig took root and thrived, and the girl was able to sell cuttings from her plant at such high prices that she was soon able to gather together sufficient money for her lover to be able to marry her.

This delightful story is commemorated by Tuscan girls, who still wear a posy of jasmine on their wedding day.

Lily. The lily is especially connected with the Virgin Mary, and appears regularly in Italian religious painting.

The story of its origin comes from Spain, where lived a poor widow who had one son. He was a simple though good boy, and it troubled her that he was unable to learn anything. Eventually she took him to the nearby monastery and asked the monks if they would care for him and try to teach him. They tried, but were unable to make him remember any of the lessons they set him; as the boy was so patient and so good, however, they kept him in their midst. After long hours working on the land he would go to the chapel where he would kneel for hours before the altar. The monks watched and listened to him and discovered that all he ever said during his long vigils was 'I believe in God, I hope for God, I love God'. Then one day he did not come from his cell in the early morning, and there the monks found him lying dead on his bed of straw, on his face an expression of great joy and peace. The monks buried him and erected over his grave a beautiful marble cross on which was inscribed 'I believe in God, I hope for God, I love God'. Shortly afterwards a lily appeared from his grave, and when the grave was opened it was found that the lily sprang from the very heart of the boy.

Lily of the Valley. An old legend tells that lily of the valley flowers first sprang from the blood of St. Leonard when it was shed during his struggle with a dragon in Horsham Woods in Sussex. It is not difficult to believe this story on beholding the delicate little flowers growing in the shady depths of St. Leonard's Forest when spring lays its finger on the Sussex woods.

It is the lily of the valley which is supposed to draw the nightingale into the heart of the woods to choose its mate.

Marigold. Shakespeare records the marigold's habit of opening its petals with the rise of the sun and closing them with its setting in his lines:

> The Marigold that goes to bed wi' th' sun
> And with him rises weeping.

Moss Rose. One day, the angel who sprinkles the flowers with dew slept peacefully in the shade of a rose bush. As dusk fell the angel awoke, and caressing the bush she said: 'Thank thee for thy cool shade and refreshing perfume. I will willingly grant thee any favour thou may ask of me.' The spirit of the rose bush thought carefully and then replied: 'The favour I would ask is that you should endow me with a new charm.' The angel instantly adorned the flowers with the beautiful moss they now bear, from which they derive their name.

Motherwort. The longevity of the inhabitants of a village in Japan was attributed to the abundance of motherwort which grew around it. Eventually the villagers conceived the idea of concocting a drink from the flowers which they named 'zakki', and which acquired a great reputation of lengthening life. The month when the flowers bloomed in greatest profusion was named after them, and a festival held on the ninth day.

Narcissus. One day the handsome Narcissus stooped to quench his thirst in a clear stream. He was so spellbound by the reflection of his beautiful features that he could not tear himself away from the spot, where he gradually pined to death, and the flower sprang from his body where it lay.

Orange Blossom. Orange blossom has played a leading part in the ornamentation of the bride at her wedding throughout the ages, and the choice of this flower for the traditional bridal wreath may have originated in the act of Juno in giving the fruit of the tree to Jupiter on their wedding day.

Our Lady's Bedstraw. This delicate flower is said to have filled the manger in which the Infant Jesus was laid. It is also believed to have made a bed in the stable for Mary, and that it derived its name from its part in the Christmas story.

Pennyroyal. Pennyroyal also has a connection with the Nativity. In Sicily little children put the flower in their beds on Christmas Eve, for they believe that the plant first came into blossom at the moment that Jesus was born.

Periwinkle. An old superstition tells us that the little periwinkle will inspire love.

Primrose. The ancient name for this flower was paralisos— named after the handsome son of Flora and Priapus, who died of grief for the death of Milicerta his betrothed, and was preserved by his parents when they caused the flower to spring from his body.

Purple Orchis. The dark markings on the purple orchis are said to be from the drops of blood which fell from the Cross. This belief has undoubtedly led to the name of 'Gethsemane' by which the purple orchis is known in Cheshire.

Ragwort. The Irish belief that the fairies ride to their revels on the ragwort is perhaps the reason why in Ireland this flower is better known as 'the fairies' horse'.

Rose. The rose family has always been a favourite through-out the generations, and in bygone days was in such demand and held in such esteem that it was accepted as rent in lieu of money.

It is said that to dream of roses is a portent of great good fortune. Rose dreams also foretell of love.

In Germany and Scandinavia roses are considered to be under the special protection of the fairies and elves.

Rose of Jericho. This flower is closely associated with the Holy Family. It is thought to have sprung from the earth to mark their footsteps during their flight into Egypt.

The rose of Jericho is supposed to have first bloomed at Christ's birth, to have closed at His crucifixion, and opened again at the Resurrection.

Rosemary. There is a saying which runs 'In those gardens where rosemary flourishes the lady rules the home'. Whether this is true is perhaps a question for debate, but the fragrant rosemary is widely cultivated in modern gardens. It is said that it was first introduced into England by monks who cultivated it for its curative powers, and in bygone days the roast beef of Christmas was garlanded with rosemary. Even to this day it is widely used for medicinal, cosmetic and culinary purposes.

St. John's Wort. Many are the myths and legends attached to the St. John's wort, some of them fanciful, some with a basis of fact. Certainly the plant is endowed with healing properties and is often better known as 'wound balm'. It also supplies a very rich purple dye.

The red spots are supposed to have appeared on the leaves on the day St. John the Baptist was beheaded. In some areas of France and Germany the peasants garland their doors and windows with bunches of the flowers on June 24th, St. John's day. On this day, too, peasant girls in many parts of the world hang the flowers over their doors and sleep with them under their pillows to foretell their future husbands.

Apart from its healing qualities, the plant was in bygone times considered to have the power to drive off evil spirits, and in Scotland particularly the flowers were carried to ward off witchcraft and enchantment.

Inhabitants of the island of Jersey were extra careful after sunset to avoid treading on the St. John's wort, for if they did they were in danger of being confronted by a fairy horse which would carry them about all the night through.

Along with many other flowers the St. John's wort has long been associated with lovers, and in Denmark two of the plants are placed between the ceiling beams, one plant being named after the girl, one after the boy of her choice. If the two plants grow together it is said to be a sure sign of a marriage between the two.

Scarlet Pimpernel. The gay little pimpernel is known in country places by the name of shepherd's weather glass owing to its obliging habit of closing its petals at the approach of rain, thus giving the observant countryman fair warning of the weather in store.

Snowdrop. Anyone who has examined the exquisite and delicate beauty of the snowdrop can well believe the story that it took its form from the breath of an angel on a snow-flake. Dedicated to the Virgin Mary, on February 2nd, when the image of Mary is removed from the altar, snowdrops are put in its place.

Sowthistle. This is said in Russia to belong to the Devil.

Stitchwort. This little flower is another of those said to be a special favourite with the fairy folk. In Devon it is particularly associated with fairies, and country people hesitate to pick it for fear of being followed by pixies who will play tricks on them.

Sunflower. It is widely believed that this impressive flower turns its face to follow the sun. This idea most likely sprang from the myth that Clytie was greatly loved by Helios, but he later transferred his affections to Leocothoe, daughter of King Orchamus. Having tried all ways to win back Helios, Clytie in desperation told the king of his daughter's love affair. In his wrath he had his daughter entombed alive. Helios now turned completely against Clytie, and in her misery she lay upon the earth for nine days and nights without food or drink, her eyes continually following the sun. The gods watching her pine away so pitied her that they turned her into a sunflower.

Tulip. Anyone who has heard that tulips are the fairies' cradles will doubtless look carefully into each flower before gathering it to avoid kidnapping any sleeping fairy babes!

Venus's Looking-glass. Venus possessed a mirror which had the quality of beautifying whatever it reflected. One day Venus dropped her mirror and a shepherd picked it up. He became so entranced by the reflection of his handsome face that he quite forgot his nymph. Cupid was very angry at such behaviour, and immediately shattered the mirror and transformed the fragments into the flowers we now know by the name of Venus's looking-glass.

Violets. According to mythology Io assumed the form of a white heifer to escape the fury of Juno, and in order to provide food for Io Jupiter caused the first sweet violets to spring from the ground.

Violets have always been held in high esteem for their medicinal properties and for their lovely perfume.

It is thought that the first sherbet of the Mohammedans was made from a blend of violet flowers and sugar.

Wallflower. In the Middle Ages, wallflowers were worn by troubadours as a sign of their unchanging affection.

White Campanula. Associated with the saints, this flower is known in many places as the little staff of St. Joseph.

Wild Clematis. Perhaps more widely known as traveller's joy, owing to the fact that it is regarded as the wayfarer's flower. It is also often called old man's beard because of its soft fluffy seeds with which it garlands the autumn hedgerows. Field-mice love to line their nests with the seeds, which make a soft and warm hide-away for their little families.

Wild Thyme. This is the emblem of courage. In Greece the scent of wild thyme is associated with the gods.

Wood Anemone. This is yet another flower which the fairies are supposed to put to good use – this time as an umbrella in wet weather.

Wood Sorrel. Better known in Wales as fairy bells, owing to the legend that the fairies are summoned to their woodland revels by the ringing of the bell-shaped flowers.

RAGGED ROBIN

A man of taste is Robinet, a dandy,
  spruce and trim;
  Whoe'er would dainty fashions set should go
    and look at him.
Rob scorns to wear his crimson coat as
  common people do;
He folds and fits it in and out, and does it
  bravely too.
Oh! Robin loves to prank him rare with fringe,
  and flounce and all;
Till you'd take him for a lady fair just going
  to a ball.
Robin's a roguish, merry lad; he dances
  in the breeze,
And looks up with a greeting glad to the
  rustling hedgerow trees.
How civilly he beckons in the busy
  Mrs. Bee;
And she tells her store of gossiping o'er his
  honey and his glee.
All joy – all mirth – no carking care, no
  worldly woe has he;
Alack! I wish my lot it were to live
  as happily!

ANON

CHAPTER 3

The Rose
of England

It would be a pleasure indeed if we in this small island could claim the genesis of the exquisite flower which we call the rose.

The fact remains, however, that most of the glorious blooms which adorn our gardens today are actually descendants of the varieties which grew long ago in Persia and India. Along with so many other flowers they found their way to England by way of Syria, Greece and the Mediterranean shores, eventually being transported by the Romans through France. Every phase of the journey added some new feature to the development of the rose, and there seems little doubt that at some stage the plant was cultivated in ancient Damascus, a region of rich and beautiful flowers, and there acquired the name of damask rose.

As we can well imagine, the Romans had no small influence on the history of the rose, and there were no half measures in the uses to which they put it. The Romans, like the Greeks, perfumed their homes and temples with the flowers, hanging garlands upon the walls and strewing petals thickly about the

floors. Extravagant feasts were enhanced by the presence of
the blooms in every possible guise. Tables were decorated
with them, and food garnished with their petals. Rose
wreaths were hung about the necks of guests, and crowns of
roses were even worn upon their heads to prevent drunken-
ness! Roman brides, too, were crowned with roses, but for a
different reason, this custom being linked with the garlanding
of the goddess Flora. Progressive in all things, the Romans
were far from satisfied with the rose as it came to them from
the East, and set about its cultivation with the object of
developing new varieties.

Pliny expressed doubt as to whether England derived the
name of Albion (by which it was then known) from its
white cliffs or from the masses of white roses which did, and
still do, grow here. Certainly the Romans associated the
name with *albus* (meaning 'white'), although Albion may
be a Celtic word.

Although the countless varieties of garden rose descend
from roots in foreign fields, there is little doubt that the
wild 'dog' rose that adorns the English countryside with
delicate tints from white to deepest pink is the true rose of
England, being a pure native of this land. The wild rose has
appeared in royal badges and orders since the thirteenth
century, and Crusaders carved rose emblems upon the
buildings which they erected during their long stay in the
Holy Land.

During the protracted War of the Roses, the Yorkists had
a white rose and the Lancastrians a red one as their badge,
and when in 1461 the fighting eventually came to an end, it
was Edward IV who united the two flowers into one with a
mixture of red and white petals and launched it as the emblem
of his country.

The English rose figured prominently in Tudor times, and is often referred to as the Tudor rose. This national emblem was used in the intricate designs worked into the plaster ceilings of the Elizabethan and Stuart periods. The motif invariably appeared in the centre of the ceiling, and may have been an extension of the custom of suspending a rose over the conference table when a secret conclave was held. For the Jacobites it had a special significance for they always held their secret meetings 'under the rose'. Word was passed that a secret meeting was to be held by the simple remark 'sub rosa'. Those concerned knew exactly where a rose appeared above a table, and therefore knew also without further explanation where the secret conclave would be, and in this way the wild English rose became a password and secret sign in the plotting of history.

Throughout the turbulent periods of English history the English rose was the national emblem, and was incorporated in crests and royal arms. As time progressed this dainty flower of the English wayside was used more widely, and the motive was gradually introduced into such things as coins of the realm, postage stamps and various official documents.

The rose family played a small but significant part in the French people's struggle for freedom. When the Romans introduced the rose into France, a perfume industry was quickly established, and manufacturers of the rose perfume speedily amassed considerable fortunes. With this money they were able to buy certain privileges from the king, and such privileges in later years became the rights of the guilds who had purchased them.

In England too the perfume of the rose was considered very desirable, and Henry VIII had a special perfume for his own use which was based on equal parts of rosewater and rose oil to which were added minute quantities of musk and ambergris. Methods of perfume extraction have altered little with the passage of time, and the industry still owes much to the exquisite fragrance of the rose.

Apart from perfume roses have held a special place in medicine since earliest times. Hippocrates included roses among his 'simples', and later herbalists have extolled their virtues. Taken in the morning and at night they were said to 'strengthen the hearte and take away the trembling thereof'.

Culpeper devoted much writing to the uses for roses, and in his *English Herbal Enlarged* of 1653 he wrote: 'What a pother have authors made with Roses. What a racket have they kept. I must add, Red Roses are under Jupiter, Damask under Venus, White under the Moon, and Province under the King of France. Both white and red Roses are cooling. Red Roses do strengthen the heart.'

Generations of housewives have made such concoctions as honey of roses for the treatment of sore throats and vinegar of roses as a cure for headaches, and today roses appear in the British and other pharmacopoeias.

During the privations of the Second World War, when the import of oranges was severely curtailed and the growing of fruits rich in Vitamin C was reduced in favour of arable farming, it was discovered that the fruit or 'hips' of the wild rose contained the vitamin in far larger quantities than any other source. Unfortunately the composition of the hips made it almost impossible for the housewife to use them to advantage in their original form. The central seeds are covered with stiff bristly hairs which are a danger to the internal system should they be swallowed, and as it is extremely difficult to remove the hairs completely by hand it became necessary to devise a scheme whereby the precious vitamin contained in the hips could be extracted and presented to the nation in an acceptable form.

Research and experiment produced the syrup which became universally known as rose hip syrup, and to produce this in sufficient quantity it became necessary to collect vast amounts of the hips for processing. Collecting parties from all over Britain were organized to collect the rose hips from the hedgerows after the flowers had bloomed and faded, leaving behind the rich harvest that did so much to supplement the diet of a nation at war. Thus once again the shy English rose played a vital part in the history of the country of its birth.

Much has been said and written of the rose family down the ages, but John Gerrard aptly summed it up when in 1597 he wrote:

The Plant of Roses, though it be a shrub full of prickles, yet it had been more fit and convenient to have placed it with the most glorious flowers of the world than to insert the same among base and thornie shrubs; for the Rose doth deserve the chiefest and most principal place among all flowers whatsoever; being not only esteemed for his beautie, vertues and his fragrant and odiferous smell, but also because it is the honour and ornament of our English Sceptre, as by the conjunction appeareth in the uniting of those two most royal houses of Lancaster and Yorke. Which pleasant flowers deserve the chiefest place in Crowns and Garlands, as Anacreon of Teos, a most ancient Greek poet, affirms.

With which remarks I am sure rose lovers everywhere will wholeheartedly agree.

CHAPTER 4

The Language of Flowers

The origin of the meanings attached to flowers is lost in antiquity, but it was the Victorians who developed the language of flowers to its finest art. Thoughts which could not be voiced in the presence of the chaperon were expressed in the posies which the beaux of the period presented to the young ladies of their choice.

The posies were artistic expressions of romantic thoughts, carrying within their scented petals the hopes and dreams of the gay gallants, and every damsel of that day knew by heart the meaning of every flower. Its combination with others and the manner in which the posy was arranged and presented to her spoke volumes, and if the message demanded a reply the recipient was mistress of the use of her eyes and her fan to convey her answer.

The pace of modern life and the emancipation of women have long since killed the practice of the flower language. We ourselves may never expect to employ it in the same manner as our ancestors, but it is possible, and indeed probable, that it played an effective part in our own family tree.

FLOWERS AND THEIR MEANING

Almond Blossom	Hope
Alyssum	Worth beyond beauty
Amaryllis	Pride
Anemone	Forsaken
Apple Blossom	Temptation
Apricot Blossom	Doubt
Arum	Ardour. Zeal
Balm	Sympathy
Balsam	Impatience
Belladonna	Silence
Betony	Surprise
Bluebell	Constancy
Bramble	Envy
Broom	Humility
Buttercup	Ingratitude
Camellia	Perfect loveliness
Camomile	Energy in adversity
Candytuft	Indifference
Canterbury Bell	Acknowledgment
Carnation (red)	Alas for my poor heart
China Aster	Variety
Chrysanthemum (red)	I love
Chrysanthemum (white)	Truth

Clematis	Mental beauty
Clover (red)	Industry
Clover (white)	Think of me
Columbine	Folly
Convolvulus	Bonds
Cowslip	Winning grace
Crocus	Abuse not
Cyclamen	Diffidence
Daffodil	Regard
Dahlia	Instability
Dandelion	Rustic oracle
Daphne	Glory. Immortality
Elder	Zealousness
Everlasting flowers	Unceasing remembrance
Fleur-de-lis	Flame. I burn
Forget-me-not	True love
Foxglove	Insincerity
Fuchsia	Taste
Furze	Love for all seasons
Gardenia	Refinement
Geranium (scarlet)	Comforting
Gladiolus	Ready armed
Golden Rod	Precaution
Harebell	Submission
Hawthorn Blossom	Hope
Hibiscus	Delicate beauty

Holly	Foresight
Hollyhock	Ambition
Honeysuckle	Generosity. Devotion
Hyacinth	Sport
Hydrangea	A boaster
Iris	Message
Ivy	Friendship
Jasmine	Amiability
Jonquil	I desire return of affection
Kingcup	Desire of riches
Laburnum	Pensive beauty
Larkspur	Lightness
Lavender	Distrust
Lemon Blossom	Fidelity in love
Lilac (purple)	First love
Lilac (white)	Youthful innocence
Lily of the Valley	Return of happiness
Lobelia	Malevolence
Love in a Mist	Perplexity
Lupin	Voraciousness
Magnolia	Love of nature
Mallow	Mildness
Marigold	Grief
Marjoram	Blushes
Meadowsweet	Uselessness
Michaelmas Daisy	Afterthought

Mignonette	Your qualities surpass your charms
Morning Glory	Affection
Narcissus	Egotism
Nasturtium	Patriotism
Nightshade	Falsehood
Orange Blossom	Your purity equals your loveliness
Pansy	Thoughts
Passion Flower	Faith
Peony	Shame
Petunia	Your presence soothes me
Phlox	Unanimity
Pimpernel	Change
Pink	Boldness
Polyanthus	Pride of riches
Poppy	Consolation
Primrose	Early youth
Ragged Robin	Wit
Ranunculus	You are radiant with charms
Rhododendron	Danger. Beware
Rose	Love
Rose (Christmas)	Tranquillize my anxiety
Rose (single)	Simplicity
Roses (white and red together)	Unity

Rosemary	Remembrance
Rudbeckia	Justice
Saffron	Beware of excess
St. John's Wort	Animosity
Salvia (red)	Energy
Saxifrage	Affection
Scabious	Unfortunate love
Shepherd's Purse	I offer you my all
Snapdragon	No!
Snowdrop	Hope
Sorrel (Wood)	Joy
Speedwell	Female fidelity
Star of Bethlehem	Purity
Stock	Lasting beauty
Stonecrop	Tranquillity
Sunflower (dwarf)	Adoration
Sunflower (tall)	Haughtiness. False riches
Sweet Pea	Delicate pleasures
Sweet Sultan	Felicity
Sweet William	Gallantry
Syringa	Memory
Tansy	I declare war against you
Thistle (common)	Austerity
Thrift	Sympathy
Thyme	Activity. Courage
Traveller's Joy	Safety

Tuberose	Dangerous pleasure
Tulip (red)	Declaration of love
Tulip (yellow)	Hopeless love
Valerian	Accommodating disposition
Venus's Looking-Glass	Flattery
Verbena (pink)	Family union
Verbena (scarlet)	Unite against evil
Verbena (white)	Pray for me
Veronica	Fidelity
Vervain	Enchantment
Violet (blue)	Faithfulness
Violet (sweet)	Modesty
Wallflower	Fidelity in adversity
Water-lily	Purity of heart
Willow Herb	Pretension
Wisteria	Welcome, fair stranger
Witch Hazel	A spell
Woodbine	Fraternal love
Zinnia	Thoughts of absent friends

CHAPTER 5

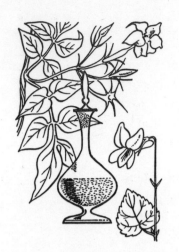

Bottled Fragrance

There must be few flower-lovers who have not at some time or other longed to capture for ever the fragrance of some particular blossom: the sharp-sweetness of lily of the valley on a May morning, the haunting perfume of tobacco flowers in the dusk of a summer's eve, the aromatic scent of thyme flowers in an old-world garden, or the elusive fragrance of a favourite wild flower. This same urge appears to have been felt by man since the dawn of civilization, and perfumes from many sources and in various guises have been used for thousands of years.

The Ancient Egyptians were very advanced in the art of perfumery, using their perfumes both in religious rituals and for cosmetic purposes. Perfumed oils and pomades, kept in magnificently carved alabaster pots and boxes, were used to anoint the bodies of Egyptian ladies during their toilette, and paintings showing these operations were found at Thebes. The anointing by slaves of the heads of banquet guests was another purpose for which these perfumed oils were used, and the walls and floors were strewn with fresh flowers to give up their fragrance as the guests moved among them.

The legend relating to the discovery of attar of roses (page 51) may or may not be based strictly on fact, but it is true that when the eleventh-century knights returned from the Crusades they brought with them gifts of rosewater for their ladies. Enchanted by its fragrance the ladies of the period soon found plenty of uses for their new acquisition, and at a time when fingers were more in evidence than forks, a finger bowl filled with rosewater was welcomed as a pleasant and dignified solution to the problem of cleansing the fingers between courses.

The Persians have always been a race with a flair for perfumes, and the preparation of rosewater has been one of their specialities since earliest times. Their original method of distilling was by boiling fresh petals in a closed pot and leading the steam off into another container. This container usually stood in running water so that the steam would quickly cool and the fragrant water settle in the vessel. Oil of roses was acquired by an equally simple method, the freshly gathered petals being packed into containers of oil of sesame and left to stand until the oil had absorbed the fragrance of the flower. The Persians' art gradually spread to other countries and Bulgaria is now famous for its attars.

Since it takes something like three dozen fresh blooms to produce one single drop of attar this is a very costly product, and care is taken over its preparation. The gathering of the blossoms is usually done in a spirit of festivity accompanied by music and laughter, and many families still follow the old method of distilling their own, but in recent years large distilleries have been erected to which the rose growers can bring their blossoms for processing.

This turn of events has a parallel in the distilling of
lavender flowers. In the years prior to the First World War
French peasants in remote regions had flourishing lavender
crops and simple distilling was carried on by each family.
This method was gradually supplanted by the visit of
travelling stills. These stills were set up in the market-places
of villages in the lavender districts and the peasants used to
gather there at harvest time with their crop. With the havoc
wrought by war such happy occasions for rejoicing faded into
the past, to be replaced by the mass production that has
overtaken so many of the old arts.

Happily for Britain we can still boast the finest lavender
in the world. Nowhere does it grow so richly and with such
abundance of colour and fragrance, and the famous Mitcham
lavender is the finest of all, commanding many times the
price of lavender from any other country. Even the renowned
perfume centre of Grasse in the Maritime Alps cannot com-
pete with Britain in this respect. The sunshine of southern
France does, however, bestow its blessing on other recipients,
and the hillsides are clothed in a riot of colour stemming
from masses of violets, jasmine, jonquils and other flowers,
each striving for predominance and challenging the pervading
fragrance of orange blossom.

The mention of Grasse invariably brings to mind visions
of vast expanses of white jasmine for which the place is
famous, and jasmine does indeed form a basis on which
many other perfumes are built.

Jasmine reacts most favourably to one of the oldest
methods of perfume extraction. Sheets of glass are covered
with a light film of fat or oil and the fresh flowers spread
over them. After standing for a day or so the old flowers are
replaced by fresh ones, and this process is repeated until the

PLATE IV   Rose (*See key overleaf*)

(facing p. 48

Moss rose

Dog rose

Bush rose

Floribunda

Modern climbing rose

oil has absorbed all it will take of the jasmine's fragrance. This method is known as enfleurage, and can be practised by any owner of a garden that harbours jasmine.

Different flowers react in different ways to various methods of extraction, and in the perfume industry each fragrance is extracted in the most suitable manner. Violets give of their best through maceration, which is in effect the process of steeping the flowers in warm fat or oil. As the flowers become exhausted they are replaced by fresh ones until the oil is fully saturated. Rosemary and lavender are subjected to boiling in water, while carnations and mimosa are often treated with volatile solvents.

The modern perfumer in his shining laboratory bears little resemblance to the perfumer of ancient times, and yet the extractions with which he strives to blend his fragrance, and the methods by which they are obtained, are basically the same as they were centuries ago. Even their names often have a strong link with the past, a classic example being oil of Neroli. This is the name given to the essence of orange blossoms and relates to the wife of the Prince of Neroli who used the oil to perfume her gloves.

Many of the pure extractions are so pungent that the exquisite fragrance of the fresh flower becomes blurred, and it is for this reason that they are blended together in varying proportions in order to capture the true perfume. The one essential that a perfumer *must* possess is a 'good nose'. Whatever his chemistry qualifications they count for little if his nose cannot recognize and *remember exactly* any given scent. Upon the perfumer's sense of smell hangs the success of his profession.

In the blending of perfumes one fragrance usually predominates. This is especially so in the flower scents and in

D

toilet waters. The famous eau-de-Cologne is perhaps the best example of the blending of a number of essences to create a 'top note' of one in particular.

Orange flower water was popular as a toilet water three hundred years ago, but it was John Maria Farina, an Italian who emigrated to Cologne in the eighteenth century, who blended the first eau-de-Cologne in the form we know it today. His perfume with a top note of orange blossom soon achieved fame, and since his day many variations have been played on his original theme. Every perfume house has its own particular recipe, but common to them all is the addition of oil of Neroli.

To all modern perfumes there is added a fixative which slows down the evaporation of the true essence and ensures a lasting fragrance. Up to the last half-century the majority of fixatives were of animal origin, two well-known ones being the scent glands of the musk deer and the costly ambergris, for which it is reputed murder has been done.

Fragrant plant resins such as frankincense and labdanum were also in use, and two of the methods of collecting labdanum in days gone by are of interest. Labdanum is secreted by hairs on the leaves of the sun roses which clothe the hillsides of some Mediterranean countries. In the old days as sheep wandered among the shrubs they collected the labdanum on their fleece and this was later combed off by the shepherds. Where sheep did not graze the shrubs were whipped with bunches of long leather thongs, and as the secretions gathered on the leather they too were scraped off.

In recent years, however, many perfumers have been attracted to the *Salvia sclarea*, better known as the clary sage, a riotous inhabitant of countries bordering the Mediter-ranean. This brilliant flower was originally the darling of the

German wine industry because of the exquisite muscatel flavour it imparted, but has of recent years been seized upon by perfumers because of the unusual fragrance of lavender and muscatel in the oil distilled from its blossoms.

All the best perfumes do not stem from the laboratories of the great perfume houses, and some of the most delightful ones have unusual backgrounds. One does not automatically associate the dedicated life of a monk with the making of perfume, but the monks of Caldy Island off the Pembroke-shire coast have a thriving perfumery. There in the peaceful shelter of the monastery they tend the soil and grow the flowers which they themselves harvest and distil to create a fragrance of a sweet freshness equal to any of its kind.

The story of perfume is a fascinating one, the long fingers of its history parting the mists of time, and always drifting through the ages is the fragrant breath of flowers.

✻   ✻   ✻

ATTAR OF ROSES

When the Mogul Emperor of Persia, Jehan Ghir, married Princess Nur-jehan, he commanded that a canal should be cleared in his garden and filled with rosewater. As he and his bride walked beside the fragrant water Nur-jehan noticed a scum forming on the surface. Scooping it off they found that it was of a thick oily texture and had an exquisite perfume. Nur-jehan immediately named the substance Atar-jehanghiri, meaning the perfume of Jehan Ghir, in honour of her new husband.

THE DAISY

There is a flower, a little flower,
With silver crest and golden eye,
That welcomes every changing hour,
And weathers every sky.

The prouder beauties of the field
In gay but quick succession shine,
Race after race their honours yield,
They flourish and decline.

But this small flower, to nature dear,
While moon and stars their courses run,
Wreathes the whole circle of the year,
Companion of the sun.

It smiles upon the lap of May,
To sultry August spreads its charms,
Lights pale October on its way,
And twines December's arms.

The purple heath, the golden broom,
On moory mountains catch the gale,
O'er lawns the lily sheds perfume,
The violet in the dale.

But this bold floweret climbs the hill,
Hides in the forest, haunts the glen,
Plays on the margin of the rill,
Peeps round the fox's den.

Within the garden's cultured round,
It shares the sweet carnation's bed;
And blooms on consecrated ground
In honour of the dead.

The lambkin crops its crimson gem,
The wild bee murmurs on its breast,
The blue-fly bends its purple stem,
Light o'er the sky-lark's nest.

'Tis Flora's page—in every place,
In every season, fresh and fair,
It opens with perennial grace,
And blossoms everywhere.

On waste and woodland, rock and plain,
Its humble buds unheeded rise;
The rose has but a summer's reign,
The Daisy never dies.

MONTGOMERY

53

CHAPTER 6

Flower Wines

Country wines – and flower wines in particular – have for centuries held a special place in the English way of life. Unfortunately, since the development of industrial and city life, this fine old craft has almost died out among town dwellers. Happily, though, in many country places, and in families where the craft has been passed down from mother to daughter for generations, these wines are still made; their bouquet as exquisite and their potency as vigorous as any produced from the grape.

Some of the more remarkable exponents of the crafts guard their secrets as closely as the crown jewels, but for the newcomer to the art of making flower wines there are many recipes that give delightful results. The methods are simple and straightforward, do not require special equipment, and can be carried out in any ordinary kitchen.

The rules are very simple but they do make a difference to the results, so it is advisable to pay attention to the little things.

First, gather the blossoms when they are fresh and not

overblown, and pick them as soon as possible after the dew has dried on them.

Avoid gathering during a spell of wet weather as flowers which have been saturated for any length of time do not produce good wine.

Flowers growing close to main highways collect large deposits of fumes and dirt thrown up by motor vehicles, and apart from the excessive cleaning entailed these deposits detract from the purity of the flowers, so gather blossoms that grow as far from the beaten track as possible.

Pick over the flowers gently and carefully, discarding all stems and leaves.

Measure the quantities while the petals are dry, and then swish them lightly through fresh cold water to clean.

Use clean, strong bottles for the wine, and to avoid any chance of a bottle bursting through excess fermentation *never* use a bottle of the screw-top type.

The following recipes, while still being great favourites with many experienced producers of flower wines, can be tackled by any novice in the knowledge that even the first attempts will be successful.

❀　　❀　　❀

RED CLOVER WINE

2 quarts of red clover blossom (stripped of all green)
4 quarts boiling water
2 oranges
3 lemons
4 lb. white sugar
1 oz. yeast on a slice of toast

Place the blossom in a large container and pour over the

boiling water. Leave to stand until the liquid has cooled to lukewarm.

Meanwhile wash the fruit and cut into slices.

Add the sliced fruit and the sugar to the cooled blossom and water mixture.

Spread the yeast firmly on to a slice of toast and place on the surface of the whole mixture.

Allow to stand for five days, stirring gently twice each day. On the sixth day strain off the liquid and allow it to stand still for five more days.

Strain carefully through very fine muslin and let the now clear liquid stand for three days. On the next day bottle carefully and place the corks very loosely in position. Stand the bottles in a cool place for ten days and then press the corks well down into the bottle necks.

Red clover wine should not be used for at least one month after the final corking.

❀　　❀　　❀

COLTSFOOT WINE

2 quarts coltsfoot flowers (stripped of all green)	1 orange
	3 lb. white sugar
4 quarts water	1 lemon
½ lb. raisins	1 oz. yeast on toast

Place flowers and raisins into a large container together with the rind from the orange and lemon.

Place the water, sugar, and juice from the fruit into a pan and bring to the boil. When boiling pour this mixture over the flowers and stir thoroughly. Allow to cool, then add the yeast spread on a slice of toast and leave to stand for four days.

On the fifth day, strain liquid off into a cask or other suitable container, and leave uncorked until fermentation subsides.

Finally, cork well and store.

Coltsfoot wine should be stored for at least six months before using.

※   ※   ※

DANDELION WINE

3 quarts dandelion pips	1 oz. yeast on toast
4 quarts water	3 lb. white sugar
Juice and rind of 2 lemons and 1 orange	1 lb. raisins

Bring the water to the boil and pour it over the flowers. Allow to stand for three days, stirring once every day.

On the fourth day, add the sugar and the rind of the fruit.

Boil all together for about one hour and then add the fruit juice and raisins. Allow to cool. Add the yeast on the toast.

Cover the container and let it stand for three days.

On the following day, strain off the liquid and allow to stand for three days.

Strain the liquid again and then bottle.

Place the corks only lightly in the bottles until fermentation subsides.

Finally, press the corks down firmly and store.

Dandelion wine should be allowed to mature for six months before using.

GORSE WINE

2 quarts gorse flowers   1 oz. yeast on a slice of
   (stripped from their stems)   toast
4 quarts water   3 lb. demerara sugar
1 orange   2 oz. root ginger
1 lemon

Put flowers, water and ginger in a large pan and simmer gently for twenty minutes. Add the sugar and stir until it is all dissolved.

Wash the fruit and slice it before adding it to the cooling liquid.

When the mixture is barely lukewarm, place the yeast on the toast on top of it.

Cover the container and leave to stand for six days. On the seventh day skim the surface and leave to stand again for another two days.

Strain carefully into a cask or other suitable container and allow to stand until fermentation subsides.

Add a few raisins and then cork down tightly.

Gorse wine improves with keeping, and should be stored for at least a month before using.

❊   ❊   ❊

COWSLIP MEAD

4 quarts cowslip flowers   2 lb. honey
4 quarts water $\frac{1}{4}$ oz. yeast
1 lemon

Place honey and water in a pan and simmer for one hour, skimming as necessary.

Measure off one pint of the resulting liquid and add to it the sliced lemon.

Pour the remaining liquid over the flowers and allow to stand in a warm place for one day.

On the second day add the lemon liquid and the yeast.

Allow to stand for four days and then strain.

Leave to stand for one more day, then strain off into a cask or other suitable container.

Cork and store in a cool place.

Cowslip mead should be allowed to mature for six months in the cask before bottling; it improves with age.

NOTE. Buttercup mead is made by following the above instructions but substituting buttercup flowers for the cowslips.

❋ ❋ ❋

CHAMPAGNE

2 large elderflower heads (gathered when in full bloom)	2 tablespoonfuls white wine vinegar
4 quarts water	1½ lb. white sugar
	1 lemon

Wash the lemon and grate off the rind, taking care not to include the pith.

Put the grated rind together with the squeezed juice into a bowl.

Add the sugar and pour over it the vinegar.

Add the cold water and stir all together.

Put in the elderflower heads and cover the container.

Allow to stand for thirty-six hours and then strain off the liquid.

Strain again through very fine muslin until the liquid is perfectly clear.

Bottle and cork well, leaving about two inches' clear space above the liquid in each bottle.

Store in a cool place.

Elderflower champagne improves as it matures, and the longer it is kept the more it resembles the true champagne.

❋   ❋   ❋

HAWTHORN BRANDY

Gather sufficient hawthorn flowers to fill a jar when all the green has been removed from them.

Put the cleaned flowers in the jar and fill it up with brandy.

Leave in a warm place for one month.

Strain off the liquid through fine muslin and bottle at once.

Cork well.

NOTE. Hawthorn brandy has a distinctive flavour and can be used at once.

FLOWERS FOR THE BEE

Come, honey-bee, with thy busy hum,
To the fragrant tufts of the wild thyme come,
And sip the sweet dew from the cowslip's head,
From the lily's bell and the violet's bed.
   Come, honey-bee,
   There is spread for thee
   A rich repast in wood and field,
   And a thousand flowers
   Within our bowers
   To thee their nectar'd essence yield.

Come, honey-bee, to our woodlands come,
There's a lesson for us in thy busy hum;
Thou hast treasure in store in the hawthorn's
      wreath,
In the golden broom and the purple heath;
   And flowers less fair,
   That scent the air,
   Like pleasant friends drop balm for thee,
   And thou winnest spoil,
   By thy daily toil,
   Thou patient, thrifty, and diligent bee.

From *Poetry of Flowers*
ANON

CHAPTER 7

Flower Cookery

The gourmet never tires of trying new dishes and it is seldom that the cook wearies of using novel ingredients, so it is surprising that in this modern age the flowers that add so much in colour, flavour and goodness to our table are invariably ignored. Even those who care little for the technicalities of the culinary art will agree that the addition of a bouquet of sweet herbs gives a certain distinction to the plainest stew. If these simple herbs can work such wonders, they are little compared with the miracles that can be wrought by the introduction of flowers to gastronomy.

In bygone times, when the English festive board groaned beneath a multitude of mouth-watering dishes, flowers had an important part to play, and marigold petals were an indispensable ingredient of soups and mutton dishes. The goodness these flowers impart was no greater centuries ago than it is today, and their addition to stews and other dishes towards the end of cooking time adds much in colour and flavour. The petals are equally good fresh or dried, and the town dweller who keeps a jar full of dried ones is no less

fortunate than the garden owner who takes the petals from
the plant to the pot.

Most of us know the piquant flavour of pickled nasturtium
seeds, but how many garnish our salads with the tangy
leaves and flowers, adding not only flavour but colour to a
plain green salad.

Violets and primroses too are far richer in vitamins than
many of our popular salad ingredients, as our ancestors well
knew. Medieval knights feasted regularly on rose and primrose stew, followed by venison garnished with marigolds
and accompanied by violet and onion salad, and one can
almost envy them the colour and gaiety of such a tempting
meal.

The petals of the yellow chrysanthemum blanched in
salted water make a wonderful garnish for egg and sea-food
dishes, while marrow flowers stuffed with a savoury mince
and baked in the oven are much more original than the
inevitable rissole.

For the sweet tooth there is a galaxy of exciting dishes
using all the fragrant flowers whose flavours are equalled
only by their perfume.

For those who have not the time or opportunity to distil
their own flower waters most herbalists and many chemists
can supply rose, violet, elder and orange flower waters.
Orange flower water is an indispensable factor in royal icing,
and rosewater improves all plain glacé icings, while a little
of any of the flower waters beaten into the mixture adds an
out-of-this-world touch to the simplest sponge cake.

Flower-scented sugars prepare themselves and have a place
in every cook's cupboard. All that is required of the cook is
to fill some screw-top jars with caster sugar and into each
jar push a few sprigs of the chosen plant. Into one jar should

go two or three scented geranium leaves, into another a sprig of rosemary and so on. Lavender, bayleaf, rose and vanilla are but a few of the flavoured sugars which add a distinctive note to many cakes and puddings.

The child who revolts at milk pudding can rarely resist when the offending dish is liberally laced with a favourite scented sugar, and plain bread and butter quickly acquires favour when the butter has been kept closely covered with rose petals for a few hours. If such bread and butter should also happen to be spread with rose petal jam there is no limit to the quantity which can be consumed!

The addition of rose-flavoured cream to fruit salads, ice-cream and layer cakes imparts a unique flavour and a touch of luxury.

For all rose recipes the old-fashioned, heavily scented garden varieties should be used. Many of the modern varieties, though exquisite in shape and colour, have sacrificed much of their lovely perfume.

Aromatic vinegars had a place in every old-time stillroom and on every feminine dressing-table. Laboratory-produced cosmetics have dislodged them from the toilette, but they still have a place in modern culinary art and when used with discretion add an intriguing touch to salad dressings. The method for producing violet vinegar is given on page 69, and other aromatic vinegars can be made in the same manner by substituting pinks, lavender, tarragon and other plants as desired.

No preserve cupboard is complete without its cherished stock of rose petal conserve, and apple jelly acquires a special flavour if a few sprigs of lemon thyme or other scented leaves are included for a few minutes during the boiling process.

Jasmine *Carnation*

Plate V   Fragrant Flowers

(facing p. 64

Woodruff

Old-fashioned rose

Violet

Cowslip

Clove pink

Rosemary

Geranium

PLATE VI Flowers for Cookery

(facing p. 65

CONSERVE OF ROSES

Gather one pound of old-fashioned red or pink roses. (If circumstances enforce the use of modern roses choose the most strongly perfumed varieties and nip off the hard white base of each petal.) Boil three pounds of sugar and one pint of water gently together to form a syrup. Add the rose petals together with the juice of two lemons and one dessert-spoonful of rosewater. Simmer all together until the conserve thickens, then pot and seal as usual.

VIOLET HONEY

To one pound of fresh honey add a handful of clean picked violet petals. Place in a double boiler over a gentle heat until the honey has acquired the violet flavour to taste.

Strain carefully and pot.

SYRUP OF VIOLETS

Into a quart of cold water put a quart measure (well packed) of violet petals. Place over a very gentle heat in a thick pan, and allow to steep until the colour and flavour of the petals are absorbed into the water.

Strain through fine muslin and to a quart of the violet water add four pounds of sugar.

Place in a thick pan and gradually bring to the boil, scumming as necessary, and continue to boil gently until a thick syrup is produced.

E

CONSERVE OF VIOLETS

Beat together in a stone mortar fresh picked violet petals with twice their weight in sugar. Beat till perfectly smooth and then pot and seal.

✳   ✳   ✳

COWSLIP CREAM

Gather the flowers when they are newly in bloom. Pick off only the yellow part of the flowers.

Place a pint of cream in a double boiler, add two handfuls of the picked flowers and simmer gently. Add icing sugar to taste and simmer till thoroughly dissolved.

Strain well and return to the pan.

Add the yolks of two large eggs and heat gently, stirring all the time, until the mixture thickens.

✳   ✳   ✳

PICKLED COWSLIPS

Boil together one pound of sugar and one pint of wine vinegar until a thin syrup is formed.

Place one pound of clean picked cowslip flowers into a deep bowl and pour on the boiling syrup.

Stir thoroughly together and when cool put the pickled flowers into jars and seal.

✳   ✳   ✳

CONSERVE OF LAVENDER

Strip lavender flowers clean from their stems.

Place some of the flowers with three times their weight in sugar in a mortar and beat together until fine and smooth.

Transfer to a bowl. Repeat this process until the required amount is obtained.

Stir all the contents of the bowl thoroughly together and then pot and seal.

❊   ❊   ❊

ROSEMARY HONEY

To every pound of honey add four ounces of clean picked rosemary flowers.

Simmer very gently until the honey has acquired rosemary fragrance to taste.

Strain thoroughly and pot and seal.

❊   ❊   ❊

SYRUP OF RED ROSES

Place a thick pan over a gentle heat and into it put red rose petals which have been clipped free from the white base. Cover with fresh cold water and leave to steep until the petals begin to lose their colour.

Strain the petals from the water, squeezing them out well.

Add fresh petals to the water left in the pan, and repeat this process four more times (six times in all).

Strain the liquid carefully through very fine muslin and measure.

To every pint of rosewater add one and a quarter pounds of icing sugar.

Return to the pan and boil gently to a thick syrup.

Strain and bottle for use.

NOTE. The deepest red and the most highly perfumed roses should be gathered for this syrup, so that the brightest and most fragrant results may be obtained.

RED ROSE VINEGAR

Put a pint of white vinegar into an ovenware vessel, and into it put four handfuls of red rose petals. Cover closely.

Steep in a warm oven for six hours.

Strain well and cool.

Pour the vinegar into clean bottles into which have been put half a dozen fresh red rose petals.

Cork and store.

※   ※   ※

CANDIED ROSE PETALS

Put some caster sugar into a pan with a very little rosewater. Bring to the boil and continue to boil until the syrup reaches candy height.

Remove from heat and dip the clean fresh rose petals into the sugar candy, leaving them for a few minutes to absorb it. Take each petal out carefully by its base tip and allow all surplus sugar to run from it.

Dip the moist petals one by one into a little dry caster sugar and spread out carefully to dry and crystallize.

To store the candied petals spread them out evenly between sheets of greaseproof or waxed paper and keep in an airtight tin.

※   ※   ※

VINEGAR OF CLOVE PINKS

Place one ounce of the petals in a wide-mouthed jar and cover with sixteen ounces of wine vinegar.

Allow to stand for fourteen days, and then strain through fine lawn and bottle.

VIOLET VINEGAR

Gather sufficient violet flowers to half-fill a jar when all the green has been stripped off.

Place the flowers in a jar and then fill it up with boiling white wine vinegar.

Allow this to stand for one week, and then strain off the liquid carefully, bottle it and cork the bottle well.

NOTE. Violet vinegar lends a special flavour to salads, and a stronger violet flavour may be achieved if desired by allowing the flowers to stand in the vinegar a longer time before straining.

❋   ❋   ❋

CONSERVE OF ROSEMARY

To every pound of rosemary flowers add two and a half pounds of loaf sugar. Beat together in a mortar adding a few flowers and a little sugar at a time.

When a perfectly smooth mixture is obtained turn into small pots and seal.

❋   ❋   ❋

CONSERVE OF BETONY

This is made in exactly the same manner as conserve of rosemary, but using betony flowers in place of rosemary.

❋   ❋   ❋

SYLLABUB OF ROSES

Beat two or three egg whites until very stiff and forming peaks. Gradually beat in conserve of red roses (page 65) until the mixture acquires the consistency of thick cream.

Serve chilled in glasses.

MARIGOLD CHEESE

Method 1. Beat marigold petals in a mortar until the juice can be poured off. Strain the juice into cream cheese and mix well.

Method 2. Mix whole fresh petals lightly into cream cheese. Form into little pats and strew the top of each pat lightly with a few fresh petals.

❈ ❈ ❈

WOODRUFF CAKES

Boil one pound of sugar to candy point. Remove sugar from heat and stir in a small handful of woodruff flowers. Return to the heat and bring to boiling point again.

Turn the candy into greased swiss roll tin and cut into squares before it becomes cold.

NOTE. The quantity of flowers used to each pound of sugar may be varied according to taste.

❈ ❈ ❈

TO CANDY ROSE PETALS
a sixteenth-century recipe

Dissolve refined, or double refined, sugar or sugar candy in a little rosewater, boile it to a reasonable height, put in your petals when your sirup is either fully cold, or almost cold, let them rest herein till the sirup have pearced them sufficiently, then take out your flowers with a skimmer, suffering the loose sirup to run from them as long as it will, boile that sirup a little more and put in more flowers as before, divide them also, then boile all the sirup which remaineth and is not drunke up in the flowers, to the height of manus Christi,[1] putting in more sugar if you see cause but no more rosewater, put your flowers therein when your sirup is cold or almost cold and let them stand till they candie.

*   *   *

TO MAKE SYRUPE OF ROSES
a seventeenth-century recipe

Take Damaske Roses, cut off the white of them and take six ounces of them to every pinte of faire water, first well boyled, scummed, let them stand; wring out the roses and put new in eight times; wring out the last and you have a good syrupe.

*   *   *

TISANES, CORDIALS AND SYRUPS

The very names tisane and cordial conjure up visions of the spacious days when ladies in rustling gowns had both the time and the inclination to make the most of nature's bounty. They knew intimately the healing powers of the medicinal tisanes and the refreshing flavours of those drunk merely for pleasure, and they turned their knowledge to good account.

The present trend towards complicated drugs and factory-bottled brightly coloured drinks has resulted in modern generations almost completely losing touch with natural food and healing. Pleasant though they are, the strongly flavoured 'fizzy pops' and squashes lack the subtle charm of

---

[1] The modern explanation would be to boil the syrup until it spins a thread when a spoonful is lifted from the pan. This can usually be achieved at a temperature of approximately 230° F.

the delicately flavoured tisane and cannot be mentioned in the same breath as the robust cordials and fragrant syrups of a bygone age.

Whether the over-stimulated modern palate is capable of identifying the delicate tones of a true tisane is a point in question, but for the flower-lover who would like to experiment nothing could be more simple to prepare. Simply infuse a teaspoonful of the chosen flower or leaf in a large cupful of boiling water. Allow to stand for about fifteen minutes, then stir and strain through very fine muslin or lawn until the liquid is clear. Never over-infuse as this destroys the delicate aroma and often imparts a bitter taste.

Suitable plants to use are lady's bedstraw, bergamot leaves, costmary petals, gorse flowers, golden rod leaves, hyssop, lavender and rosemary.

The syrups can be diluted to taste and drunk on their own or used to flavour other drinks. They also add interest to fruit salads and beaten into cream as a sponge-cake filling.

Meadowsweet beer makes a most refreshing summer drink, but the brandy cordial should be taken with the utmost discretion!

❊   ❊   ❊

SOPS-IN-WINE (Carnation Syrup)

Pour five pints of boiling water on to three pounds of petals from which the white base has been removed. Stand for twelve hours. Strain the liquid from the petals until it runs clear, and then dissolve two pounds of icing sugar into every pint of liquid, heating gently to ensure a good syrup.

NOTE. Strongly perfumed carnation petals produce the best syrup.

SYRUP OF STOCKS

Macerate for twenty-four hours two pounds of stock petals in five pints of distilled water. Strain the liquid from the petals until it runs clear, then dissolve two pounds of icing sugar to each pint of liquid to form a syrup.

✽ ✽ ✽

MARIGOLD BRANDY CORDIAL

Loosely fill a jar with marigold petals and fill up with brandy. Cover closely and leave for twenty-four days. Strain brandy from petals and add pure honey to taste.

NOTE. The petals may be left to stand in the brandy for a longer period if a more distinct flavour is desired.

✽ ✽ ✽

MEADOWSWEET BEER

Place two ounces each of meadowsweet, betony, raspberry leaves and agrimony in a large pan. Cover with two gallons of water and boil all together for fifteen minutes.

Strain through fine lawn and add two pounds of white sugar to the resulting liquid. Dissolve thoroughly over gentle heat.

Leave to get quite cold. Bottle.

NOTE. For those who like a sharp tang to a summer drink a little yeast spread on a slice of toast may be floated on the surface of the liquid and left overnight. In this case the yeast should be added prior to bottling, and the liquid re-strained. Care should be taken to see that all fermentation has subsided before pressing the corks home in strong bottles, otherwise excess fermentation could cause the bottles to burst.

CHAPTER 8

Flowers in Cosmetics

Many of the simple recipes used so successfully by our grandmothers are still widely used in the country. The following are all very simple to prepare and effective in use.

❊   ❊   ❊

ELDERFLOWER WATER

To one pint of boiling water add half a pound of freshly picked elderflowers which have been stripped from their stalks. Cover the container closely, place it in a pan of boiling water and allow it to simmer gently for three hours. See that the water in the pan does not boil away, and top up if necessary. Let the flower water cool and then strain through very fine muslin. Rinse bottles out with eau-de-Cologne after they have been well washed and pour in the strained flower water. If an eggcupful of eau-de-Cologne is added to each pint of flower water before bottling it will keep for several weeks.

This flower water is an excellent tonic for most types of

skin. For very dry skins omit the eau-de-Cologne and make only sufficient to last two to three weeks.

❋   ❋   ❋

COWSLIP BATH

Put into a muslin bag three handfuls of cowslip flowers. If fresh flowers are not available, dried ones may be used. Place the bag of flowers in a small bowl or basin of very hot water and leave for fifteen or twenty minutes. Transfer the bag to the bath water and use it to massage the body. This treatment is soothing and beneficial to the skin, and adds a delightful perfume to the water.

❋   ❋   ❋

LIME OR VERBENA BATHS

Add half a pound of lime or verbena flowers to a pan of boiling water, using sufficient water to cover the flowers well. Continue to simmer for about ten minutes before straining the liquid into the bath water. This extract of flowers may be made and bottled for later use, but should not be kept for more than three or four days.

❋   ❋   ❋

CAMOMILE TEA

Add two heaped teaspoonfuls of camomile flowers to a large cup of boiling water. Leave to stand for ten minutes.
This provides an excellent skin tonic and hair rinse.

❋   ❋   ❋

HOLLYHOCK COMPRESS

Add a good handful of hollyhock leaves to a pint of boiling water. Boil until the liquid is reduced to one cupful.

Cut a 'mask' from a piece of linen or cotton material and soak it in the liquid. Squeeze out surplus moisture and then spread the mask over the face. Leave it in place for at least ten minutes.

This compress is excellent for soothing sunburnt or wind-roughened skin.

❋　　❋　　❋

ROSE SKIN TONIC

Add two ounces of red rose petals to one pint of wine vinegar and stand in a warm place (preferably in sunlight) for a fortnight. Strain and bottle.

This makes an excellent toilet water for use on the body after bathing.

❋　　❋　　❋

VIOLET SKIN TONIC

This should be made in the same manner as the rose tonic, but substituting violet petals for the rose petals.

❋　　❋　　❋

BUTTERCUP OINTMENT

Into a small saucepan put half a pound of pure white vaseline and press into it as many buttercup flowers freshly stripped from their stems as it will absorb. Place over a gentle heat and keep at simmering point for one hour. Be careful not to let the ointment come to the boil.

Remove from heat and immediately strain through fine muslin into clean pots or jars. Allow to set before putting on tops.

This is used by country people as a healing cream for all types of sore and rough skin.

ELDERFLOWER OINTMENT

This is made in the same manner as buttercup ointment and is fine as a remedy for chapped skin and for the treatment of 'heat bumps'.

❀ ❀ ❀

ELDERFLOWER HAND SALVE

Simmer one pound of elderflowers in half a pound of unsalted pure lard until it turns pale green. Strain through fine muslin into pots.

Gardeners find this salve cleansing, healing and softening.

❀ ❀ ❀

LILAC OIL

Strip the flowers from freshly picked sprays of lilac and place in a bowl. Cover with almond oil. Leave in a warm place for a fortnight (preferably in the sun). Stir at intervals. Squeeze out the flowers and strain and bottle the oil.

This oil is very soothing if applied warm to sore skin, and a few drops added to creams or to the bath will impart a delightful perfume.

❀ ❀ ❀

DRYING SUMMER FLOWERS FOR WINTER USE

Gather the flowers early in the morning while the dew is still on them. Strip them gently from their stems and spread out evenly on large sheets of paper. Cover them with a piece of muslin to keep them free from dust while allowing the moisture to evaporate. Place them in a warm, airy place and turn the flowers or petals gently every day. When they are all *thoroughly* dry pack them into airtight jars and store in a cool, dark cupboard.

A sixteenth-century recipe to make water of apple blossom for the complexion

'When the bothes begynne to blossome and to go open, then shall be layde a fayre lyne cloute underneathe the appell tree and bete upo the braunches of the tree with a small stycke and the leues of the flowres whiche as than fall downe gadered and dystylled in balneo marie.'

A rough translation would appear to be that one should lay a linen sheet beneath the apple trees when the buds begin to open, beat the branches with a stick to make the petals fall, and distil the petals so gathered to make a flower water for washing the face.

❋   ❋   ❋

A sixteenth-century recipe for a complexion water made from lavender flowers

'Take a gallon of faire water, one handfull of Lauender flowres, and few cloues, and some orace powder,[1] and foure ounces of Benjamin;[2] distill the water in an ordinarie leaden still.'

❋   ❋   ❋

A recipe from 'The Toilet of Flora' *to make orange flower water*

'Take four pounds of unpicked orange flowers, bruise them in a marble mortar and pour on them nine quarts of clear water. Distil in a cold still and draw off five or six quarts which will be exquisitely fragrant.'

[1] Orris root (from the iris).
[2] A vegetable gum used as a fixative to slow down the evaporation of the perfume.

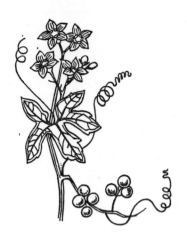

CHAPTER 9

Pot-Pourri

One of the great joys of a garden is that its fragrance can be captured to live on long after the last bloom has faded. When logs crackle on the hearth, and snow blankets the sleeping earth, a bowl of pot-pourri will revive golden memories of summers past, and bear rich promise of those still to come.

The making of pot-pourri is a delightful task, and one so simple that the least experienced cannot fail to produce a perfect and lasting fragrance. The secret of success lies in the gathering and drying of the flowers, and if possible they should be picked during a warm spell of weather. Half-open buds will retain their fragrance and colour far longer than full-blown flowers, and these should be picked in the morning soon after the dew has dried on them. Care should be taken not to bruise the petals during gathering and drying.

Drying trays can be made by covering wire cake-trays with butter muslin, or otherwise by lining empty shoe or other cardboard boxes with paper. Flowers must be spread in *thin* layers on the trays and placed in a warm, airy place

for ten days. An airing cupboard with the doors left slightly
ajar is an excellent drying place, and the flowers should be
turned very gently once every day. At the end of ten days
the flowers and petals will be dry and ready for blending.

Much pleasure can be derived from experimenting with
different blends, and the addition of about one tablespoonful
of powdered orris root (obtainable from the chemist) and
one tablespoonful of common salt will improve and preserve
the fragrance. A few drops of jasmine, lavender or other
flower oils may also be blended in, and the addition of spices
lends an exotic note.

Use a large bowl to blend the flowers in. Place the chosen
flowers in the bowl and mix them thoroughly, then add the
salt and orris root and mix again. Sprinkle on any flower oils
to be used in the blend before giving the pot-pourri a final
mix and packing lightly into the containers.

Any covered container can be used for the pot-pourri, but
pretty glass jars look most attractive filled with the multicoloured petals. Keep the lids in place to preserve the
fragrance, removing them for an hour or two during the day
to let the perfume steal out into the room.

The following are some simple blends, each with its own
distinctive fragrance. The number and variety of blends are
legion, and experiment will produce the perfume most
pleasing to individual taste.

English Bouquet. One pint of lavender flowers, petals from
one dozen red roses, petals from one geranium, one teacupful
sweet-scented stocks (multicoloured), one teaspoonful allspice, one tablespoon common salt, one tablespoon orris
root.

Sweet Lavender. Two pints lavender flowers, few drops
lavender oil, one tablespoon common salt.

Cottage Garden. Two pints red rose petals, one geranium, one teacupful sweet-scented stocks, six rose geranium leaves, two fern leaves, one sprig of lemon thyme, one sprig of rosemary, one teacupful lavender flowers, one teaspoon ground cloves, one tablespoon common salt, one tablespoon orris root.

Verbena. Two pints lemon verbena leaves, half-pint lavender flowers, few drops lavender oil, one tablespoon common salt.

Mystic East. One pint rose petals, one tablespoon lavender flowers, one tablespoon crushed and dried orange peel, one teaspoon ground nutmeg, one teaspoon allspice, two dozen whole cloves, one tablespoon common salt, one tablespoon orris root.

Summertime. One pint mixed rose petals, one teacupful lavender flowers, one teacupful carnation petals, one tea-cupful marigold petals, petals from four pinks and one dozen mixed stocks or night-scented stocks, few drops jasmine oil, one tablespoon common salt.

❊   ❊   ❊

PERFUMED SACHETS

A Victorian linen cupboard was not complete without its lavender sachets, and their omission from present-day cup-boards has served only to deprive us of the blissful relaxation almost magically induced by fragrant bed linen. It seems a pity to deprive ourselves of such pleasure when it is a matter of moments to make the little flower-filled bags which bestow that elusive perfume.

The contents of each sachet are indicated by personal taste, but lavender, rose petals or verbena leaves lend a

F

deliciously fresh fragrance acceptable to almost everyone. Various blends of pot-pourri may also be used to fill sachets intended for wardrobes and lingerie drawers, while lavender or verbena leaves are most refreshing in handkerchief drawers.

The flowers are dried in the same manner as for pot-pourri, and any odd scraps of thin material may be used to make the little bags. More ambitious creations fashioned from satin, muslin or organdie and trimmed with ribbons make attractive and welcome gifts.

✳   ✳   ✳

SOME OLD RECIPES [1]
Damask Powder – 16th Century

Five ounces orace, two ounces cipres, two ounces calamus, half an ounce cloves, one ounce benjamin, one ounce rose leaves, one ounce storax calamitum, halfe an ounce spike flowers, mix them well together.

Sweet Bags for Linen – 18th Century (Mrs. Glasse)

Eight ounces coriander seeds, eight ounces sweet orris root, eight ounces damask rose leaves, eight ounces calamus aromaticus, one ounce mace, one ounce cinnamon, half an ounce cloves, four drachms musk powder, two drachms white loaf sugar, three ounces lavender flowers, and some rhodium wood. Beat all well together, and make into silk bags.

[1] The ingredients of the recipes for perfumed sachets consisted of these herbs, spices and woods, sometimes in natural form, sometimes as powders, together with the essences, sugars and fixatives, and although we might find them rather pungent today they were very popular during the sixteenth to eighteenth centuries.

Perfume for Gloves – 16th Century

One pound rose petals, one pound orris root, half an ounce benzion, half an ounce storax, five ounces calamus, three ounces citron essence, one ounce coriander seeds, half an ounce lavender, four ounces rosewood.

❊   ❊   ❊

TWO OLD RECIPES FOR PERFUMING A ROOM
17th Century

One glassful of rosewater, a pennyweight of cloves beaten to a powder; make a pan red-hot on the fire and put in the powder and rosewater. The mixture will evaporate little by little to give an excellent odour. (Or so it was thought at the time.)

A Royal Perfume
By Queen Anne's Confectioner. 1719

Take three spoonfuls of perfect rosemary and as much sugar as half a walnut beaten into small powder; all these boyle together in a perfuming-pan upon hot embers, with a few coals.

BROOM

On me such beauteous summer pours
That I am covered o'er with flowers;
And when the frost is in the sky
My branches are so fresh and gay
That you might look at me and say—
'This plant can never die.'

The butterfly, all green and gold,
To me hath often flown,
There in my blossom to behold
Wings lovely as his own.

WORDSWORTH

Spring goeth all in white,
  Crowned with milk-white May!

ROBERT BRIDGES

Buttercup, the little children's dower.

ROBERT BROWNING

The Snowdrop in purest white array
  First rears her head on Candlemas Day.

DAFFODILS

Faire Daffodils, we weep to see
  You haste away so soone:
As yet the early-rising Sun
  Has not attain'd his Noone.
    Stay, stay,
Until the hasting day
    Has run
  But to the Even-song:
And having pray'd together, we
  Will go with you along.

We have short time to stay, as you,
  We have as short a Spring;
As quick a growth to meet Decay
  As you, or any thing.
    We die,
As your hours doe, and drie
    Away,
  Like to the Summer's raine;
Or as the pearles of Morning's dew
  Ne'er to be found againe.

ROBERT HERRICK

CHAPTER 10

Pollination and
Seed Dispersal

Research into the rhythm of evolution has uncovered an extraordinary train of events in the methods of pollination and reproduction, and because of the remarkable connection in the development of plants and insects reproduction of the species is perhaps more interesting in plant life than in any other.

In earliest times pollination was ensured by insects, who in search of nectar transferred the pollen from flower to flower. Doubtless scent and colour were the attractions for most insects, but in the mysterious way of nature certain flowers formed a close alliance with certain insects, and to accommodate their favourites and keep marauders at bay each plant family gradually developed flowers of highly individual shapes. With the passing of time new and beautiful flower shapes were evolved and a close link between flower and insect was established, and today we can watch various little winged creatures hovering about their favourite blossoms, their tongues matching exactly the length of the calyx from which they sip the nectar.

The pink family holds a special attraction for some butterflies, and the busy bumble bee seems happiest when he is diving head first into the deep bells of the foxglove, his furry back and rump smothered in pollen. Some of the richly coloured flowers of the tropics are pollinated by hummingbirds, and in the Java jungles even the bat does his share towards the work of pollination.

All pollination, however, is not carried out in this way. Some flowering trees and grasses rely for the most part upon the wind to carry their pollen, extra-long stamens ensuring that pollen is easily gathered by the breeze and carried to the seed-bearing flowers. Self-pollinating species have a system which is remarkable for its simplicity. These flowers have anthers raised high above the stigma on to which they shed their pollen, and the pollen is then drawn down until it reaches the ovary and the future seed.

Irrespective of the method by which pollination takes place, the next step in reproduction is the ripening of the seed, and this process continues until the seed reaches maturity and is ready to produce the next generation of the species.

Just as nature evolved certain methods for pollination, so she has devised systems for seed dispersal. Wind, water, birds and animals each play a part, while in some cases the plants themselves disperse their own seed by means of shaking or expulsion.

Wood sorrel, violets and vetch are three plants which burst their seed pods with a sharp explosion, scattering the seeds around, and the poppy family distribute their own seed by lifting the top of the seed pod and shaking out the contents in all directions. The seeds of traveller's joy or old man's beard sail on the wind, as do dandelion and other downy seeds. Other seeds such as those of the scabious have little rounded bases which help them to bounce along the ground like miniature shuttlecocks, while the seeds of some water-loving plants are carried by the streams into which they are dropped.

Birds eat rose hips and other fleshy seed pods and carry the seeds for great distances, while plants such as the burdock ensure widespread distribution by producing little hooked seeds which catch on to the coats of passing animals – and sometimes the clothes of human beings – to be cast off in far places. Many plants, including a large number of our garden annuals, endeavour to ensure their reappearance on the same scene by dropping their seeds where they stand – a habit which some gardeners do not always appreciate.

So by one means or another seeds reach their new resting place to await germination, and once again the scene is set for a new generation, a new colony to spring up and play its part in the mysterious plan which ensures the preservation of the species.

THE WILLOW HERB

June stopped a moment in a city street,
Then fled dismayed from the drab haunt of men,
But in the wake of her capricious feet
Beauty has come again.

For on this stretch of rubbish-laden ground,
Between grey houses and the muddy curb,
Lifting tall heads with misty glory crowned,
Blossoms the Willow Herb.

Afar it flings a splash of radiance bright
When the heat quivers in the sunny hours,
But evening finds a cool mysterious light
Entangled in its flowers.

Eyes brighten as they catch the sudden glow,
And little London children stand and stare,
Wondering to think how even June could throw
Such wealth of colour there.

FLORENCE LACEY

CHAPTER II

Sports and
Rarities

If you are a keen gardener you may already have known the surprised delight of finding a sport among your own lovingly tended plants, or if you are a country-lover, addicted to communing with nature at close quarters and in out-of-the-way places, you may have experienced the thrill of discovering one or more rarities of British flora.

If not, then these are two pleasures yet to come.

RARITIES

The simplest country walk becomes a grand adventure when there is always the possibility that growing somewhere along the way is one of the flowers that are unfortunately becoming all too rare. Hikers and ramblers by the dozen may have passed it without a glance, but for those who care its discovery makes the day. These rarities, in common with some bird species, have a habit of suddenly reappearing in places from whence they have long since disappeared, proof indeed that Mother Nature is ever watchful of her own, and most unwilling to allow any member of her vast family to depart for ever. The appearance of some old and almost forgotten flowers on London's bombed sites is evidence that time means little to nature in her staunch devotion to the task of renewing herself, and this should restore hope to the flower-lover who regrets the near-disappearance of many of our most attractive wild flowers.

There are two methods of seeking rarities. One is to keep a vigilant eye open at all times in the hope of accidentally finding a blossom in an unexpected place, and the other is to set out deliberately to seek them in their most likely haunts.

For some unexplained reason the orchid family have a distinct fascination for rarity seekers, though they are not in fact the rarest of flowers. Between 1953 and 1957 new colonies of the military, the monkey and the ghost orchid were discovered, the ghost orchid up to that time being considered the most rare, having been recorded during only eight years between 1854 and 1953. Since the new colonies have appeared the ghost orchid has been seen each year and has now been surpassed by the lady's slipper as the star rarity among orchids. The ghost orchid, with its pale yellow mauve-lipped flower, is difficult to find in the deepest shade of the Chiltern woods where it appears from the end of May to the end of August, but the reward is there for the diligent seeker. Lady's slipper, on the other hand, is a dashing maiden clad in red and yellow reigning in solitary dignity atop her graceful stem in rare corners of Yorkshire.

In Suffolk and the Chilterns the military orchid may be sought for, its pale mauve hood, striped inside with deeper mauve, and its carmine-spotted lip being its hallmarks, while the monkey orchid with its pale monkey-like flowers appears in Kent as well as the Chilterns.

By the less observant the rare Loddon lily may be mistaken for a very large snowdrop. Known also as summer snow-flakes, these exquisite flowers appear only in damp meadow-land beside the Thames. The even larger spring snowflake, though often appearing in gardens, grows wild only in one or two damp places in south-west England during February and March. Another flower that is common to gardens but rare in its wild state is the grape hyacinth. Favouring dry grassland, these tiny blue blossoms may be sought for in the Cotswolds and East Anglia.

The purple-red wild gladiolus rejoices only in the quiet corners of the New Forest, while the higher rocky ledges of Snowdonia give sanctuary to the Snowdon lily, whose purple-veined white bells give such pleasure to those for-tunate enough to discover them in bloom during May and June. The glory of the wild peony is ample reward for the flower-lover who ventures from Weston-super-Mare by boat to rocky Steep Holm in the Bristol Channel, and the landlubber in the Weston-super-Mare district will find joy in the sight of the pure white rock rose.

Visitors to the Cheddar Gorge during June and July cannot fail to be thrilled by the lovely Cheddar pinks which adorn the rocky ledges. These are the rare variety *Dianthus gratianopolitanus,* clove-scented with five-toothed petals, and not to be confused with the *Dianthus plumarius* and *Dianthus caryophyllus* which are naturalized on the walls of Beaulieu Abbey.

Many flower-lovers are astonished by their first sight of intensely blue spring gentians growing in limestone areas of northern England, having believed these flowers to be a Swiss speciality. Although comparatively rare in England, the spring gentian is in fact fairly common in western

Ireland, and its smaller sister appears in a few high places in the south-eastern Highlands of Scotland.

Native only to Scotland and now very rare indeed is the exquisite St. Olaf's candlestick, its lovely fragrance and the purity of its waxy white petals laying a spell of wonder and delight on the few who are fortunate enough to find it. Less difficult to find during May and June in coastal areas of Devon, Cornwall and South Wales is the garlic-scented white bluebell with its characteristic three-cornered stem and green-striped white bell flowers, while to the Bath area spiked star of Bethlehem lends its delicate beauty.

Britain is rich in its flora and to the diligent seeker comes the reward of finding the rarest of the rarities. It does not fall to all flower-lovers to have either the time or the opportunity to seek the rarities in their known native haunts, but an observant eye may discover a new colony in the most unexpected place.

The search is always worth while, for if we do not actually discover a rarity there is always the thrill of finding the first shy violet of the year unfolding its fragrant petals with the ever-new promise of spring.

SPORTS

Many of our most beautiful garden flowers are sports of some simple variety and it is certain that many more have bloomed and died, lost to us for ever because no one recognized them at the time.

Close examination will show that it is rare for two flowers of any variety to be absolutely identical. The difference may be so slight that only the observant eye will notice it, but occasionally along comes a sport, one flower that is outstanding among its fellows. It may be only that it is a much

larger bloom than the rest, or of a better colour, or of more
vigorous habit. But it may have some really unusual point
about it, perhaps its shape or colouring.

The Giant Waved sweet pea is an example of this.
Originally all sweet peas were rather small with smooth-
edged petals. Then along came a flower with wavy petals.
This bloom was noticed and isolated from its fellows and its
wavy habit transferred to other varieties by crossing.

The seeds of many sports breed true from the start and
certain dwarf varieties, including the dwarf chrysanthemums
and cornflowers, are examples of true breeding. Careful
isolation of the seed from all the others is often sufficient to
ensure a new variety being bred from the sport.

Some double flower forms were sports of single varieties,
and it is well worth while for any gardener to cultivate an
observant eye so that he can recognize any valuable gift that
nature may bestow.

All new flower varieties are not the accidental product of
nature, but are in fact the result of deliberate crossing
carried out by gardeners with special interest in the art. An
Austrian monk by the name of Gregor Mendel did most of
the early work in this field, with the result that today we
know this absorbing art as Mendelism.

A complete subject in itself, Mendelism has been dealt
with in specialist books. The flower-lover with sufficient
interest in the art could find intense pleasure in closer
study, and it is not beyond the hope of any of us to produce
one of the latest wonders of the flower world!

Flower emblems for every month

January. A wreath of sweet-scented tussilago encircling a robin.

February. A garland of snowdrops encircling goldfinches.

March. A wreath of almond blossom encircling a bird's nest.

April. A garland of furze encircling a linnet.

May. A garland of hawthorn blossom encircling a nest of young birds.

June. A circlet of grasses surrounding a spray of strawberries.

July. A thick garland of purple thyme.

August. A garland of wheat, barley and oats round a cluster of plums.

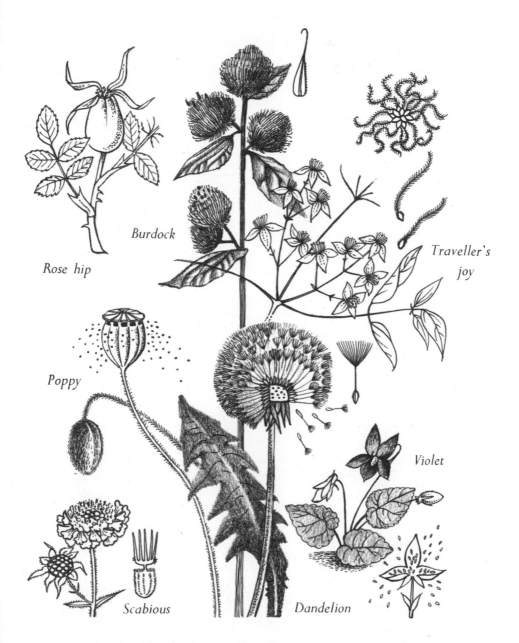

Rose hip

Burdock

Traveller's joy

Poppy

Violet

Scabious

Dandelion

PLATE VII   Methods of Pollination and Seed Dispersal

(facing p. 96

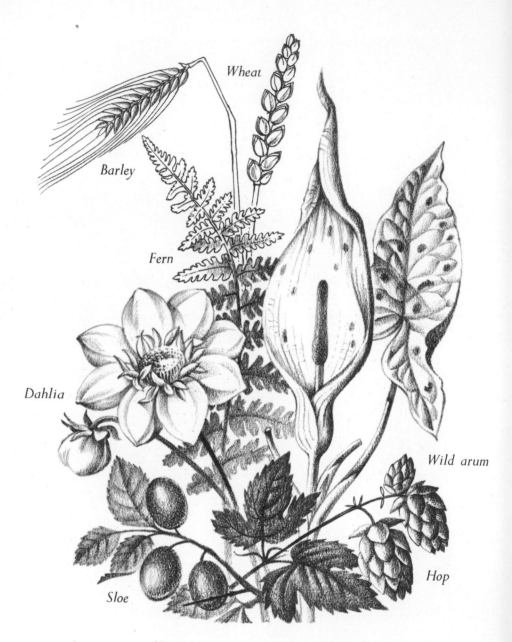

Wheat

Barley

Fern

Dahlia

Wild arum

Sloe

Hop

PLATE VIII   August Selection

(facing p. 97

September. A wreath of hops encircling a bunch of grapes.

October. A circlet of China asters around a cluster of hazel nuts.

November. A garland of ivy in flower.

December. A wreath of holly round a bunch of mistletoe.

G

CHAPTER 12

Preserving Flowers

Every flower-lover longs at some time or other to be able to keep for ever some special bloom. And in the long dark winter evenings thoughts steal away to rose gardens in full blossom, dreaming of gathering lovely bouquets to be arranged indoors. Happily, with a little forethought, these dreams can be satisfied at any time.

That very special flower will last for years if it is kept in a bottle of surgical spirit. Just place the flower in a suitable jar or bottle filled with the spirit, and after three to four days replace with more spirit and screw the top back tightly. Some flowers may lose a little of their colour over a period, but they will remain in otherwise perfect preservation for many years.

Roses 'fresh from the garden' for Christmas and winter birthdays can also be a dream come true. All that is needed is a tin box, some sealing-wax and a little care. Choose a dry day as late in the season as possible before the first frost comes to gather some half-opened rose buds. Cut each stem cleanly with a very sharp knife and immediately seal the cut end with sealing-wax. Seal each flower before cutting the next. Lay all the roses gently in the box, being careful not to crush them, and then seal the lid down tightly with more wax. Make sure that no pin hole is left whereby air could enter the tin, and then store the box away in a cool place where it will not be disturbed. When the flowers are required, unseal the box, cut off the sealed part of the stems and arrange in bowls as desired, adding a sprinkle of salt to the water, when they will bloom as magnificently as they did in high summer.

The lovely green of summer and the exquisite reds and golds of early autumn leaves will grace a room long after the boughs are bare if the stems have first been allowed to stand in a 50/50 mixture of glycerine and hot water.

The ever-popular statice and helichrysum need not be the only dried flowers to bring colour to winter vases. Many leaves and ferns have a delicacy of shape that gives point to flower designs, and the variety of tints they present when dried add interest to the arrangement. Spread the leaves carefully between blotting-paper and then enclose in news-paper before placing under a heavy weight. Large books are useful for this purpose, being flat and evenly weighted.

Long trails of bryony berries and the seed-heads of traveller's joy will last the entire winter, as will haws and rose hips. Seed-heads of many wild and garden flowers have great beauty of shape and are well worth drying (hung upside-down in a warm airy place) for winter vases.

Roses and chrysanthemums will often dry successfully if packed carefully in borax in an open box and stored in a dark place; and experiments in this manner with a wide variety of blooms often produce charming results.

MAKING CUT FLOWERS LAST

All flowers benefit from a long drink in deep water before being actually arranged, but this is absolutely essential when they are bought from a shop. Trim the stems before placing in deep water and leave in a cool dark place (overnight if possible) before arranging.

All flowers. Trim stems *under water*. This prevents air pockets forming in the tip of the stem and so stopping the flower drawing up water.

Roses. Slit the stems and leave them overnight in a deep container with water up to their heads. Arrange as desired next morning in water to which a teaspoon of glycerine has been added.

Dahlias and other flowers with juicy stems. Touch tip of stem with flame of a lighted match, or dip in boiling water.

Autumn flowers and all elaborate arrangements. Add one dash of household bleach to the water. This keeps the water fresh and prevents the unpleasant smell associated with some autumn flowers and with arrangements whose design makes it difficult to change the water regularly. 'Topping up' only can be done for several days when a little bleach is present.

Almost invariably two or three flowers remain bright and fresh when the rest of an arrangement has faded. These make pretty 'cushions' for table use and to brighten odd corners.

Fill posy rings, small bowls or saucers with sand. Cut the flower stems very short and press into the sand so that the flower heads form a little flat posy. Keep the sand moist, and the flowers can be replaced as they fade, making a continuous pattern without requiring complete rearrangement.

Some flowers appear to develop an aversion for one another's company. If a mixed vase of fresh flowers appears to be drooping unaccountably separation of the blooms into different containers will often give fresh life to them all.

A new lease of life is given to tulips and other bulbous spring flowers if, after two or three days in water, they are removed from their vases and laid on thick newspaper overnight. Arrange next morning in fresh water.

CHAPTER **13**

A Handful of Flowers

The gentle art of 'doing the flowers' was once indulged in almost exclusively by ladies of leisure who spent many hours arranging the blooms brought in fresh each morning by the gardeners. Not so today. Flower arrangements have found a place in the humblest home, and where once an earthen mug of garden-gathered marigolds brought brightness to a cottage window-sill, a bowl of shop-bought flowers now stands in formal glory.

Unfortunately, enthusiasm for this art can lead to un-happy results, and this is a pity, because the rules for success are few and simple.

The first, and perhaps the most important because it has the most immediate effect, is always to fit the flowers and their arrangement to the setting. The type of display that would give splendour to a Regency drawing-room would only look pompous in an old-world cottage, just as an arrangement designed to add graciousness to a formal dinner table would look faintly ridiculous amidst the gaiety of a children's party tea-table.

The second rule is – don't copy! Apart from adding beauty and fitting in to the setting and the occasion, flowers should express the personality of the arranger. We all have our favourite flowers, but it is the general impression of a display that makes its impact on us whatever the flowers used, and if you see something that really appeals to you, by all means use the *idea*. Look at the design as a whole and then turn away and close your eyes. It is highly improbable that you will recall which flower went where, or even how many kinds of flower were used, but the general impression will be there and this can be used as a basis on which to build up a design, using your own choice of blooms in your own way.

This method is often very helpful to a beginner, but it is the creative arrangements that give the most pleasure, and these should always be your aim.

Rule number three applies to almost every trade and art. Use the right materials for the job and keep them scrupulously clean: a very sharp, short-bladed knife; a pair of secateurs; some half-inch-mesh chicken wire and some modelling clay; one or two heavy-based pinholders; and perhaps a packet of Florapak. A collection of vessels for holding the arrangements is better acquired gradually. All sorts of containers that suggest designs can be picked up very cheaply in the most unexpected places. Junk shops and street markets are happy hunting grounds for interesting pieces, though it should always be borne in mind that the container must never distract attention from the flowers, but its shape and colour should play a part in the display as a whole. Family attics and china cupboards invariably harbour discarded oddments that are crying out to be brought into use for purposes other than those for which they were originally intended. Large tureens, pewter carving dishes, old tankards, oddments left over from a treasured tea or dinner service, crystal finger bowls, brown earthenware jugs, wooden bowls and platters and silver eggcups can all be given a new lease of life in a fresh and interesting manner.

We now come to the actual arrangement, and rule number four, which concerns proportion. Proportion is one of the worst stumbling blocks, especially for beginners, and the only way to master it is to consider the arrangement as a whole right from the beginning.

Choice of both flowers and container depends upon the circumstances prevailing at the time, but one must be in keeping with the other. Having decided upon these, shape is the next step. Basically every arrangement is built up within a shape. It could be triangular, circular, rectangular – but never square. The finished arrangement must never show the harsh outline of the basic shape, but the invisible form is the underlying framework of every successful design, and the first stems to be fixed in place should mark out the main points of the shape. For instance, a formal triangular shape in a large urn would have its highest point at top centre in correct proportion to the height of the urn, and the two side extensions marked by the lowest flowers placed on either side in horizontal positions. A fan shape on a tray or salver would be marked out in a similar fashion. Both designs, though entirely different in their finished state, would in fact have been built up from similar basic steps.

Practice and imagination are the most valuable instructors, and once proportion has been mastered there is no limit to what can be achieved.

The temptation to get on with an arrangement immediately the flowers are to hand can lead to trouble – particularly with shop-bought flowers. If possible buy or cut flowers twenty-four hours before they are wanted at their best. It is a good idea to take a bucket of water into a shady place in the garden when cutting home-grown flowers, and as each flower is cut place it there immediately. Dahlias last better if dipped in hot water after cutting and milky-stemmed flowers such as poppies like their tips singed before being placed in water; but make sure only the very *tip* is scorched. With shop-bought flowers first remove any binding and the lower leaves and cut off *under water* a small piece from each stem, then place them up to their heads in a bucket or other suitable container of water. Leave all the flowers in a cool, dark place for twelve hours before arranging them.

Have everything ready for arranging the flowers before taking them from their buckets. Fix the chosen support firmly into the container, using modelling clay to secure crumpled chicken wire, and part fill with water. Take each flower, cut to correct length – preferably under water – and place in position immediately. Woody stems should have the ends well bruised with a hammer or split for two or three inches, while hollow stems, such as lupins, will benefit from being filled with water and a finger placed firmly over the end until they are safely below water level in the arrangement. Poppies will require to be singed again to avoid 'bleeding'.

If you are a keen gardener you will doubtless prefer to grow at least some of your own flowers for decoration, and experiments prove less expensive if you have not had to pay a fortune to the florist. Plants really worth growing yourself, especially if you have a greenhouse, are the ones which bloom in the barren months when shop-bought flowers are priced at so much a bloom rather than a bunch, and out-of-season flowers, normally beyond the pocket of the majority, can be acquired by growing them at home.

If the garden area is small, use it to advantage by not growing the flowers which can be bought for a few pence a bunch at the height of the season, but concentrate on those which last well when cut, and which will be most useful from your personal point of view for decoration. Try too to grow the flowers which are not so readily available in the ordinary florist's, and be selective regarding colour when choosing plants and seeds. A good seed and plant catalogue from one of the leading nurserymen will provide all the necessary details to help make a choice suitable for your special requirements.

In choosing flowers for arrangement, do not forget nature's bounty to be found in the hedgerows. A hart's-tongue fern or a textured leaf may be the very thing to add point to a design. Hips and haws, sloes, bryony berries and the like suggest fascinating designs besides paying the dividend of making long-lasting arrangements for the autumn months. During any excursion into the country keep a lookout for things that will be useful in completing arrangements: odd pieces of tree bark, interesting twigs or branches, dry seed-heads, a pretty stone or flint, or any of the other things that are always awaiting the sharp eye.

But never be so enchanted by the sight of a carpet of bluebells as to be tempted to gather them for indoor use. They will show their misery at being removed from their natural woodland home by drooping in sad untidy heaps. Bluebells are one of our lovely wild flowers that prefer to blossom and fade in the arms of Mother Earth, and this is just as well, for their unco-operative behaviour when gathered ensures that they are left in peace to beautify the countryside.

The charm of flower arranging does not begin and end with the art itself. Interesting facts about plants and flowers can be learned along the way. Eccentricity is not confined to the human race, and flowers also have their share. For instance, violets enjoy nothing better than going into water head first; and if you allow them to drowse away the night with their heads in water they will reward you by blooming fairer than ever next day.

We can learn about colour too. Nature has an extraordinary capacity for blending the most unexpected colours, and by careful observation we can borrow from her palette to enhance our own material possessions. A posy of gleaming marigolds reflected in a silver platter may be all that is required to light up a dull corner, while a large pewter jug filled with delphiniums and placed at the turn of the stairs can transform a rather ordinary climb up to bed.

Fitting arrangements to their setting can only be accomplished by each individual, but a few ideas can help a beginner to find her feet.

Dinner tables can be tricky. Guests should be able to see one another clearly above the flowers, and the decorations should not have a chance to find their way into the food. The basic rule is to keep arrangements low.

Very formal occasions demand elegance. A damask cloth and the family silver could bask in the reflected glory of one or two perfect camellias resting on a bed of dewy moss. Tall candles rising from the midst of a circlet of fragrant freesias would solve the problem of finding space on the table for flowers *and* candlelight.

Buffets can also be a headache, but this can be overcome

by arranging the flowers in a cascade design and mounting it on the wall behind the buffet. At wedding receptions this idea can be supplemented by decorating the front of the buffet itself with looped garlands of flower heads and leaves fixed on to white ribbon with fine fuse-wire.

Wherever there are to be people gathered together in numbers it is wise to see that arrangements are placed in safe positions where they cannot be knocked over, and one or perhaps two big and beautiful designs in strategic positions are better than a lot of little insignificant bowls scattered about.

This is particularly vital where children are concerned. Out-of-reach should be the rule. Shape two pieces of chicken wire into hollow balls and fill them with damp moss. Into these push the shortened stems of a mixture of gaily coloured flowers so that the finished effect is one of large puff-balls of flower heads. These look gay, and suspended from the ceiling are out of reach of small inquisitive hands.

It should always be borne in mind that the art of flower arranging revolves round living things, and every effort must be made to avoid a wooden effect. The whole design, be it large or small, should have the appearance of life and movement. It is not necessary to have large quantities of flowers to gain this effect, as anyone who has studied the art as practised by the Japanese will know. This inscrutable race have an almost magical gift for making one single bloom, or even a bare branch, create the most exquisite and lively arrangements.

Never regard the odd couple of blooms as useless. Two irises left over from a large arrangement would make a strong impact placed firmly upright on a heavy pinholder, one bloom slightly higher than the other. Add one or two spears of self-foliage to point up the fluid lines of the petal formation, hide the pinholder by the careful arrangement of one or two stones or a piece of tree bark, and present the design on the outer edge of a shallow dish or tray, or on a piece of natural wood.

Again, when the close of the year brings chrysanthemums – beautiful but expensive – make them appear more so by practising effective economy. Use only three blooms and cut the stems to within two inches of the heads. Choose your most beautifully shaped shallow bowl and float the flower heads on the water like water-lilies. If you have only one bloom and possess a brandy glass, half-fill the glass with water and float the flower in it. This idea can be adapted for use with other flowers.

Mirror is also useful for getting extra value from a few flowers. Use the mirror as though it were a lake, and arrange the flowers close to the edge so that an interesting reflection is shown.

If, because of scarcity or price, winter puts fresh flowers almost out of reach, do not overlook the beauty of dried seed-heads, coloured barks and berries. The beautiful coloured barks of many of our trees and shrubs are a bonus that is too often disregarded; even one single branch can be so lovely that it will make a focal point for any room, and should not be spoiled by the addition of extra bits and pieces.

Sometimes the marrying of container and contents has a remarkable effect. Put laburnum in a silver jug and watch flower and silver glow even brighter. Hazel and pussy willow catkins become more delicate in the company of old pewter, and peonies take on an even greater glory in a marble urn. These are not, of course, the only containers with which these flowers can be used to effect, and experiment and a seeing eye will always produce fresh delights.

When arranging mixed colours in any quantity, care must be taken to avoid the appearance of a 'hole' in the centre when viewed from a distance. This can easily happen when dark flowers such as deep red roses are used as the focal point in a surround of delicately shaped flowers of pale colour. If this happens it can be remedied by replacing the dark flowers with lighter ones, but as this task invariably upsets the entire arrangement it is as well to bear the thought in mind at the start and choose colours that will produce a good balanced effect.

Anniversaries and festivals go hand in hand with flower decoration and offer a wide scope to the imagination. Christmas springs immediately to mind, and no flower-lover worth her salt would be satisfied with the inevitable sprays of holly drooping sadly over every picture in sight. By all means use the traditional holly, ivy and mistletoe, but use them with imagination, and always spend a few minutes polishing the leaves of evergreens if you would gain the best effect. If leaves and berries are very dirty they can be swished lightly through cold water to which a few drops of liquid detergent have been added. Rinse thoroughly in clean water before drying. A soft cloth very slightly moistened with glycerine or almond oil will add gloss to evergreen leaves.

The traditional star appears in most Christmas décor, but it is more original to make it of flowers than of silver paper and frost. Try making a large star shape from wire and damp moss and fill it with white chrysanthemum heads on two-inch stems. Put it on a table with a red candle at each point of the star. Or make only the outline of the star and place a group of candles in the centre.

Harvest suppers are a time of rejoicing for the bounty safely gathered in, and decorative materials to fit the occasion are plentiful indeed. One huge display built up from the various kinds of grain, scarlet poppies, blue cornflowers, red and gold chrysanthemums and well-polished fruit would make a focal point for the room. Garlands of wheat-ears and cornflowers lying the length of the centres of long tables would make a neat and pretty decoration without getting in the way. A large square table could take a more ambitious arrangement, and here a large copper dish might hold an arrangement of physalis (Chinese lanterns), white chrysanthemums and polished vine leaves or Virginia creeper. Sussex trug baskets filled with rosy apples, cornflowers and wheat might stand on side or serving tables.

St. Valentine's Day falls at a time of year when flowers are few and relatively expensive, but it takes only a few flowers to emphasize the symbol of the occasion. A heart-shaped basket filled with moss and scattered with a few spring flowers would make a suitable centrepiece, but if a heart-shaped cake is to take pride of place on the table make a simple rope of ivy and violets with which to surround it, or place a silver eggcup holding shreds of moss and a few snowdrops at each place-setting.

Personal anniversaries are very special occasions which depend for suitable décor on the taste of the people concerned and the time of year, but simple table decoration is nearly always the most effective. Pure white marguerites shine like stars when placed in a shallow bowl on a dark green cloth, while deep purple clematis has a delicate beauty that is enhanced against snowy damask. Clematis also looks exquisite when it is laid in natural sprays on a silver salver.

The products of nature are at once a pleasure and a

challenge, and many happy and relaxing hours can be enjoyed with just a handful of flowers.

When thinking of arrangement, after-care should not be forgotten, for the greater the care the longer the life. The two main reasons for short-lived flowers are air-lock in the stems and the growth of bacteria and algae in the water. Cutting the stems under water as referred to earlier helps to prevent air-locks, and scrupulous cleanliness of containers and other materials cuts down bacteria, while making sure that no leaves are below water level helps to prevent the formation of algae.

A little attention to the comfort of the flowers is also helpful. Do not subject them to extremes of temperature and draughts. Do not leave them to wilt on a window-ledge in blazing sunshine during the day, or to shrivel there on a frosty night. Keep mossy arrangements damp and top up vases daily with *aired* water, and change all water at the first signs of distress. In the case of stems that incline to slime wash the container thoroughly, wash the stems well and cut the tip off each before rearranging.

Invariably some blooms outlast the remainder and these can be used to make gay little cushions to put on side tables or shelves. Fill shallow dishes, posy rings, saucers or other suitable containers with clean builder's sand (not seashore sand), and add sufficient water to make it damp but firm. Cut the flower stems to within an inch of the head and push them into the sand close together to form a flowery cushion. Keep the sand moist and the arrangements will keep fresh for a long time.

Basic rules can be taught and suggestions made for designs, but the real art of flower arranging is essentially creative, a spontaneous gesture by those who love to handle flowers.

PLATE IX Sports and Rarities (*See key overleaf*)

(*facing p. 112*

Spring gentian

Military orchid

Lady's slipper

Spiked star of Bethlehem

Peony

St. Olaf's candlestick

It is sometimes desirable to plan flower arrangements well in advance, and it is helpful to have some idea of which flowers will be available at the time so that designs and quantities can be worked out beforehand without having to worry whether this or that will be to hand at the crucial moment. Every month adds its own contribution to the floral year, some blooms being more suitable for cutting than others, some blooming over long periods but being most useful indoors at certain times.

The calendar of flowers on pages 155–60 shows at a glance a selection of the flowers, foliage and other decorative materials which are readily available at certain periods of the year, and by using this as a guide it is possible to plan arrangements in advance of requirements, and by ringing the changes every week enjoy a wide variety of indoor flowers throughout the entire year.

H

Jottings from a bygone age

✳   ✳   ✳

About Lavender

I judge that the flowers of Lavender quilted in a cap and dayly worne are good for all diseases of the head that come of a cold cause – and that they comfort the braines very well.

WILLIAM TURNER, 1551

✳   ✳   ✳

About Sweet Williams

These plants are not used either in meates or medicines, but esteemed for their beauty to decke up gardens, the bosomes of the beautiful, garlands, and crownes for pleasure.

JOHN GERARD, 1597

✳   ✳   ✳

About Gilliflowers

The leaves of the flowers put into a glasse of vinegar and set in the sunne for certaine dayes, do make a pleasant vinegar, and very good to revive one after a swoon, the nostrils and temples being bathed with it.

WILLIAM COLES, 1651

✳   ✳   ✳

There be made a vinegar, or infusion of it, which being rubb'd against the nostrills is good against all contagious airs and night dews, and all effects of melancholy.

JOHN BAPTIST PORTA, 1658

About Marigolds

If ye take it out of ye earth before the arising sun, and bind it to ye body and hang it about the neck, doth good, averting the women witches, and all enchantments.

GREEK HERBAL, 1655

❋   ❋   ❋

The water of Marigold flowers is appropriate to most cold diseases of the head, eyes and stomach. They are in their vigour when the sun is in the Lion.

NICHOLAS CULPEPER, 1653

❋   ❋   ❋

MARIGOLDS

Open afresh your round of starry folds,
Ye ardent Marigolds.
Dry up the moisture of your golden lids,
For great Apollo bids
That in these days your praises should be sung
On many harps which he had lately strung.

JOHN KEATS

❋   ❋   ❋

Drink the flowers with wine to comfort the stomach and procure appetite.
Take the conserve of the flowers fasting to cure trembling of the heart and to withstand plague and the evil eye.
Bruise a marigold leaf and put it into thy nose to cleanse the head and avoid reume.
The flowers colour hair yellow.
Preservative from death, drink 111 grains of marigolds.

WILLIAM LANGHAM, 1578

About Daffodils

The double white Daffodil of Constantinople was sent into England unto the right honourable the Lord Treasurer, among other bulbed flowers whose roots when they were planted in our London gardens did bring forth beautiful flowers, very white and double, with some yellowness mixed in the middle leaves, pleasant and sweet to smell.

JOHN GERARD, 1597

❃   ❃   ❃

About Rosemary

Carry powder of the flowers about thee, to make thee merry, glad and well-beloved of all men. Lay the flowers on thy bed to keepe thee from all evill dreames. The conserve of the flowers comfort the hearte marvellously.

Take the flowers and put them in a rosewater, seethe it and drink it to comfort the hearte.

WILLIAM LANGHAM, 1578

❃   ❃   ❃

If thy legges be blowen with the gowte boyle the leaves in water and then take the leaves and bynde them in a lynnen clothe about thy legges and it shall do ye moche goode.

Boil the leaves in whyte wyne and wasshe thy face therewith.

Put the leaves under thy bed and thou shalt be delyvered of all evylle dremes.

Ete the flowres with hony fastynge with sowre breed and there shall be the none evill swellinges.

Take the tymbre thereof and burne it to coles and make powder thereof and put it into a lynen cloth and rubbe thy tethe therewith and if there be any wormes therein it shal flee them and kepe thy tethe from all evills.

Take the flowres and put them in a chest amonge your clothes or amonge bokes and moughtes shall not hurte them.

Make a box of the wood and smell to it and it shal preserve thy youthe.

BANCKE'S HERBAL, 16th Century

✽   ✽   ✽

About flowers generally

Who would look dangerously up at Planets that might safely look downe at Plants?

JOHN GERARD, 1597

There is not a Herb here below, but he hath a star in Heaven above.

THOMAS VAUGHAN, 17th Century

✽   ✽   ✽

And because the breath of flowers is far sweeter in the air (whence it comes and goes, like the warbling of music) than in the hand, therefore nothing is more fit for that delight, than to know what be the flowers and plants that do best perfume the air.

FRANCIS BACON

✽   ✽   ✽

The flower glorifies God and the root parries the adversary. Flowers are peculiarly the poetry of Christ.

The doubling of flowers is the improvement of the Gardener's talent.

The Lord made a Nosegay in the meadow with his disciples and preached upon the lily.

CHRISTOPHER SMART, 18th Century

THE PARTI-COLOURED ROSE, OF SOME NAMED
YORKE AND LANCASTER

The Rose in the forme and order of the growing is neerest unto the ordinary damaske rose, both for stemme, branch, leafe and flower, the difference consisting in this, that the flower (being of the same largenesse and doublenesse as the damaske rose) hath the one halfe of it sometimes of a pale whitish colour, and the other halfe of a paler damaske colour than the ordinary; this happeneth so many times, and sometimes also the flower hath divers stripes and markes in it, one leafe white or striped with white, and the other halfe blush or striped with blush, sometimes also all striped or spotted over, and other times little or no stripes or markes at all, as nature listeth to play with varieties in this as in other flowers; yet this I have observed, that the longer it abideth open in the sun, the paler and fewer the stripes, markes or spots will be seene in it; the smell whereof is of a weake damaske rose scent.

THE GARDEN OF PLEASANT FLOWERS, 1629

CHAPTER 14

Making Flower Pictures

Fashions in pictures move with the times. The past fifty years alone have witnessed an amazing assortment of picture fashions, including stags at bay and highland cattle knee deep in cloud-shadowed lochs, to say nothing of likenesses of frock-coated bewhiskered gentlemen whose penetrating stare seemed to follow one about the room in a most disconcerting manner.

Present generations have staged a minor revolt against such ponderous décor, preferring perhaps one well-chosen specimen to blend with the current trend towards light and airy interiors. Tastes vary considerably and depend to some extent upon the type of furnishings the chosen picture is expected to complement.

Unfortunately for the seeker of flower prints, the somewhat restricted selection does not always produce a picture with exactly the right atmosphere about it, and in this respect do-it-yourself enthusiasts have a wonderful opportunity of expressing their own creative and artistic ability with the real thing. Forgetting the usual materials of paint, brushes and canvas, look instead to the flower world. Any flowers, leaves or grasses that will dry well can be used to make the most delightful pictures, from the contemporary style of simple shapes to the lush arrangements more suited to the pretty 'chintzy' room.

Gather the flowers, etc., while they are young and fresh, and spread them carefully between sheets of blotting paper, then place under a heavy flat weight (books will do quite well) until all moisture has been absorbed by the blotting paper and the flowers are dry and firm. Autumn tinted and skeleton leaves may be successfully used by holding dry or fallen leaves in a little steam to make them supple again and then pressing very gently with a warm iron. Seed-heads, too, add interest to the picture, and if necessary these can be treated in the same way. When collecting flowers and leaves look for interesting shapes and colours and choose those which will make the type of picture most suited to the room it is to grace.

While the flowers are drying collect together the materials for mounting and framing. Colour and type of background mount should be given careful consideration if the flowers are to be seen to advantage. Black and very dark greens or blues provide an excellent background for the pale neutral tones of seed-heads and light-coloured skeleton leaves. Pure white or delicate pastel tints complement the richer colours of autumn leaves.

The simplest picture frames are best for this type of picture. Anything heavy or ornate only serves to distract the eye from the delicate beauty of flower shapes. Junk shops will often produce good frames which can be titivated with a little paint, or a simple frame can be made to measure quite cheaply. The only other materials needed are a little rubber solution and some transparent sticky tape.

Cut the background mount to fit the glass in the picture frame exactly. Then cut an extra piece of plain paper to match the size of the mount. On this second sheet arrange the flowers, etc., moving them around until a satisfactory design is achieved. Single leaves or seed-heads arranged in an abstract pattern may be preferred to a posy-like composition, but the secret is to get the picture exactly right before proceeding further.

Place the first background mount on a firm flat surface, and then taking one flower or leaf at a time from the second mount fix it in the identical place on the first mount by means of one or two *tiny* blobs of rubber solution touched to the back at suitable points. Press very gently into position.

When the design is complete, lay the freshly cleaned glass over it and bind the two surfaces firmly together by fixing sticky tape carefully round the edges, making sure that the tape will not show beyond the inner edge of the frame when it is fixed into position. Finally, fix the design firmly into the frame and the picture is ready to hang.

Neutral colours of seed-heads, dried grasses, skeleton leaves, etc., are not normally affected by light, but definite coloured flowers or leaves should not be exposed too much to the fading effects of strong sunlight if the colours are to be preserved. Happily, however, a flower has the delightful habit of showing even more effectively the beauty of its shape long after its colour has disappeared.

CHAPTER 15

Green Fingers

There comes a time in the life of every flower-lover when he feels the urge to discover for himself whether or not he is blessed with green fingers.

Many would-be culturists are deterred by lack of a garden, but however restricted the opportunities there is in fact ample scope for each and every one to experience the miracle of the tiny seed bringing forth its blossom under the care of his or her own hand. Wherever there is breathing space there is room for flowers, and to the city flat dweller falls the joy of tending indoor plants and brightening the view with gay window-boxes, which with reasonable care will flourish in spite of grime and smog. Occupants of basement rooms can have fun and gaiety in their tiny walled yards by using tubs, wall pots and hanging baskets. The possessor of a tiny suburban plot is no less fortunate than the owner of spreading acres, for in the flower world there is no class distinction and for poor and rich alike every blossom uncurls its petals in the same glorious abandon.

INDOOR PLANTS

Even the city flat dweller who lacks so much as a tiny yard and whose tenancy regulations prohibit the use of outside window-boxes need not be dismayed, for to him comes the thrill of indoor plant cultivation – an occupation that has its own special advantages and delights. There are many lovely plants which thrive best in an indoor atmosphere, and plants can be bought as and when available and rearranged at will to present an ever-changing display of colour and charm.

Which plants to include in the 'indoor garden' depends largely upon individual choice, space, and suitability of atmosphere. The majority of indoor plants – even the so-called temperamental ones – will thrive happily under simple treatment that remembers to pay attention to the likes and dislikes of each plant.

All plants need light, moisture and breathing space. A sunny draught-proof window-sill suits the majority of plants provided the more tender ones are protected from cold at night, especially in winter, the simplest method being to transfer them to the centre of the room before retiring.

The best way of judging whether or not a plant needs water is to tap the side of the pot with the edge of a penny. If it rings the soil is dry, but if the sound is dull the plant has plenty of moisture. Standing the pot in a bowl of water overnight will allow the roots to take up all the water they need, but if this is not convenient careful filling with water of the space between soil and top of pot is usually sufficient. It is now also possible to buy a special 'wick' to afford the plant a permanent source of moisture, and most florists should have these in stock.

Among the less usual and certainly most interesting plants for indoor cultivation are:

Crown of Thorns. As its name suggests, this plant is believed to have played a part in the Crucifixion and it appears in many biblical paintings. The plant grows in the Holy Land today, but botanists are still not convinced that it grew there at the time of the Crucifixion. The grey stems with their long spines and sparse green leaves are interesting enough in themselves, but the bright red bracts surrounding the flowers bring gaiety to the winter scene. A sun-loving plant, crown of thorns should be protected from frost, icy draughts and damp atmospheres. With such simple care in winter, and plenty of water in summer, this cheery plant will live for many years and rarely be bare of its bright red bracts.

African Violet, or *Saint Paulia ionantha.* This was named after its discoverer, Baron Walter von Saint Paul, but is in fact not a true violet. Its rich deep purple flowers are nevertheless a delightful addition to any indoor plant display, and the leaves are easily rooted in a mixture of sand and peat or vermiculite, thus enabling the grower to increase his collection quickly and easily without additional expense. The plant loves a fairly humid atmosphere, but will not thrive near coal or gas fumes. With careful daily watering with tepid water this little plant will flower all the year round.

Orange Tree. This is a most obliging plant which produces sweetly scented flowers in May which are followed by the fruit. The plant likes light and sun, but not too much heat, and will flower for years with frequent summer and occasional winter watering.

Geranium. Of all our so-called pot plants perhaps the geranium is the best all-rounder, being equally at home in a single pot on a city window-sill or bedded out *en masse* in every type of garden, its bright colours bringing cheer and gaiety wherever it appears. The geranium is said to have acquired its rich colouring from the honour it received when the prophet Mohammed spread his shirt to dry over the common mallow. When he removed the shirt the flowers flourished in a blaze of glory. Today this plant blooms in a variety of colours from white through a range of pinks into the ever-popular scarlet and richer reds. A versatile member of this family is the ivy geranium with its glossy ivy-shaped leaves and pink flowers. It makes a pretty picture tumbling from a window-sill, cascading from a hanging basket, or spilling down from a wall pot-holder. The long pliable stems can also be trained to climb trellis against a wall or merely round a cane. The plant asks for little attention except regular watering and the removal of faded flowers and leaves, and will bloom from spring to late autumn outdoors and even longer with indoor care; and just for good measure one single plant will provide several good cuttings for rooting. The young shoots should be removed carefully with a sharp knife immediately below a leaf joint. All but the topmost leaves must then be nipped off and the cut end placed firmly into a box or pot of damp sand or a sand and soil mixture over which a layer of sand has been spread. Keep the rooting mixture damp but not over-wet, otherwise the cutting will damp off where it enters the soil.

Impatiens, or *Busy Lizzie*. Here is a plant that will not only provide a mass of flowers all the year round but has extra interest in its quick-snapping seed pods. In its original tropical East African home the flowers were brick-red, but hybridists created a wider range by hybridizing the plant with the *Impatiens sultani* from Zanzibar. The colour range now includes white, several pinks, tangerine and scarlet. The flowers show up best in good light but should not be placed in too strong sunlight. Be sparing with water during the winter but water frequently in warm weather.

Primulas. This dainty plant ranges through all the delicate pinks and mauves and with care will flower all the year round. If the leaves show signs of turning yellow or transparent, water the plant with a solution made up of half a teaspoonful of calcine sulphate of iron to half a gallon of water. For normal watering use the rule of tapping the pot with a penny to determine whether the plant requires moisture.

Azaleas. These are the plants that immortalize the work of the ancient gardeners of old Japan and China. Admired by most and despaired of by many, azaleas regularly goad their owners into complaining that they just cannot be grown indoors. The cause of this complaint is invariably the fact that so many growers do not realize that most tap water contains lime in varying quantities, which azaleas just will not tolerate. To water this plant with tap supply is usually fatal, but this obstacle can be overcome by using rain water. Azaleas grow best in a peat mixture. They delight in a humid atmosphere and should be kept well watered. When buying azaleas choose plants with plenty of buds and one or two blooms that are just opening.

Cyclamen. The ever-popular 'rabbit's ears' range from pure white through all the pinks and mauves to deep red. Keep away from draughts, do not have the soil too wet, and keep water off the corm itself. Choose plants with plenty of buds and strong dark green leaves. An important point to remember is *never* to *cut* off dead flowers and leaves. Always pull them out at the base.

WINDOW-BOXES

Ready-made window-boxes of various types and sizes can usually be obtained from local garden specialists, or a joiner will often produce one to required size for a very reasonable fee. The handyman will undoubtedly derive pleasure from making his own, and in all cases it should be borne in mind that a box should never be less than nine inches deep and six inches wide, with half-inch drainage holes spaced about six inches apart. Junk shops and scrap yards often hide antique boxes of lead or terra-cotta, but these are usually highly priced, and for all essential purposes the simple wooden box is ideal.

The most important point is to preserve the inside of the box by coating liberally with Cuprinol, a highly effective preservative which has no harmful effects on the plants such as are often experienced with creosote and other types of preservative. A good drainage must be provided to keep the soil sweet and this is best done by placing pieces of broken crock, hollow side downwards, over the drainage holes, and then placing a layer of rough broken crock over the bottom of the box. A garden specialist or nurseryman will no doubt supply the crock if otherwise unobtainable.

For the city dweller it is advisable to obtain soil from a nurseryman who will deliver suitable quantities ready mixed, and the soil should be allowed to settle for a few days in the box before introducing the first plants. The beginner would be wise to ensure initial success by obtaining young plants from a reliable nurseryman. These will be offered

either in small pots or from seed boxes. Care must always
be taken to see that the roots are not damaged in the process
of transferring young plants from seed box or pot to the
window-box, and that they are spaced out sufficiently to
allow light and air to circulate freely among them when they
reach maturity.

One of the joys of window-box gardening is that a
constant variety of colour and pattern can be achieved
throughout the year by the replacement of bulbs and plants
as the seasons roll by. To bring cheer to the early months of
the year there is a wide variety of bulbs, some of the most
useful being:

Flower	Planting Time	Depth	Apart	Blooming Time
Aconite	Sept. to Oct.	2–3"	2"	Jan.
Chionodoxa	Sept.	3"	2"	March
Crocus	Sept.	3"	2–3"	Jan. to March
Fritillaria	Sept. to Oct.	4"	3"	April to May
Daffodil	Sept. to Oct.	4–5"	3"	March to April
Muscari	Sept. to Oct.	3"	3"	March
Hyacinth	Sept. to Nov.	4–5"	2"	March to April
Narcissus	Sept. to Oct.	4–5"	2"	March to April
Scilla	Sept. to Oct.	3"	2–3"	Feb. to May
Tulip	Oct.	4"	5"	March to May

The majority of bulbs will bloom year after year if they
are lifted after the blooms have completely faded and
stored in a dry place. Alternatively bulbs left undisturbed to

Ivy-leafed geranium

Pelargonium

Fuchsia

Tradescantia

Begonia

PLATE X   Flowers for Hanging Baskets and Wall Pots

(facing p. 128

Convolvulus tricolor

Convolvulus ipomoea tyrianthina

Passion-flower

PLATE XI   Climbing Plants

(facing p. 129

multiply are a valuable addition to a permanent window-box.

With the approach of summer the seasonal window-box becomes a riot of colour and the flower-lover is hard put to decide what he shall plant from the galaxy of plants available. Between the annuals (which bloom and die in one year) and the perennials (which continue to flower for several years) only the individual can decide, but the annuals make an ever-changing seasonal display whereas the perennials provide a permanent garden.

The following lists may be of some help in making a choice and planning a colourful display.

ANNUALS

Flower	Colour	Blooming Period
Marigold	Yellow	June to Oct.
Cornflower	Blue. Pink. White	July to Sept.
Clarkia	All the pinks	July to Oct.
Candytuft	Various	July to Aug.
Dwarf sweet pea	Various	June to Oct.
Virginia stock	Pink. White	May to Sept.
Nasturtium	Red. Yellows. Orange	July to Oct.
Canary creeper	Yellow	July to Sept.

All the above annuals are easily reared from seed and ensure the novice complete success should he wish to raise his own seedlings in a seed tray before transferring to the window-box. When annuals are grown watch should be kept on the flowers and all dead ones removed before seed-heads appear. This ensures a succession of flowers over the entire blooming period.

I

PERENNIALS AND BEDDERS

Flower	Colour	Blooming Period
Ageratum	Blue	July to Oct.
Alyssum	White. Mauve	June to Oct.
Antirrhinum	Various	June to Oct.
Aster	Various	June to Sept.
Begonia	Various	June to Sept.
Calceolaria	Yellow to brown shades	July to Sept.
Campanula	Blue. White	June to Aug.
Cerastium	White	May to June
Chrysanthemum	Various	July to Oct.
Daisy	Red. White. Pink	April to June
Dianthus	Red. White. Pink	June to Sept.
Doronicum	Yellow	April to May
Erigeron	Various	May to Oct.
Forget-me-not	Blue	April to July
Fuchsia	Red. Pink. Purple	July to Oct.
Geranium	Red	June to Oct.
Heliotrope	Mauve	June to Sept.
Lily of the valley	White	May
Musk	Yellow	May to Aug.
Oxalis	Pink	May to Sept.
Pansy	Various	May to Aug.
Petunia	Various	July to Oct.
Salvia	Red	July to Sept.
Saxifrage	Pink. White	May to June
Stock	Various	April to July
Tagetes	Yellow	July to Sept.
Wallflower	Various	March to May

Once one has known the delight of a gay window-box from early spring to mid autumn, the prospect of an empty box for winter is not to be considered. Apart from the winter heaths which are an excellent stand-by, there is a wide variety of dwarf shrubs and evergreens to add interest to the box until January brings forth the first aconite again. Any good nurseryman can offer a selection of these dwarf shrubs, which are invariably grown in pots. The shrubs may be transplanted from pot to window-box, and then repotted, watered and kept in a well-ventilated place during the spring and summer until they are required to do their turn of duty at the window-sill when winter comes round again.

HANGING BASKETS AND WALL POTS

A hanging basket filled with a colourful assortment of flowers is easy to maintain, requiring only the regular attention of a watering-can and the picking off of dead flowers and leaves to ensure a long flowering season.

Simple strong wire baskets are very cheap to buy and light to handle. They should be lined with good basket moss and then filled with a medium mixture of loam, peat and sand with a little leaf-mould mixed in. The nurseryman will provide both moss and soil when otherwise unobtainable.

A basket display should be designed with a strong and colourful central plant surrounded by edging and trailing plants. A sturdy scarlet geranium is hard to beat for a focal point and round this can be built numerous interesting designs. Fuchsias and begonias are also good where softer colour is required, and the selection of edgers and trailers is almost inexhaustible.

Mesembryanthemums, nasturtiums, creeping jenny and trailing lobelia are but a few of the flowering trailers, while tradescantia, Japanese honeysuckle and *Asparagus sprengeri* are among the most popular trailing foliage. Alyssum, nepeta, musk and *Lotus peliorhynchus* will also bring interest to the basket, as will toadflax and strawberry begonia.

Before experimenting with a mixed basket the novice may prefer to try a one-flower basket. Here again the geranium is useful and effective, providing both standard and trailing varieties in a wide selection of shades from white through all the pinks to bright scarlet and deep crimson. Begonias too come in many colours and sizes, as do the fuchsias.

Once planted, care should be taken to see that the basket has plenty of moisture, and if at all possible it should be suspended in a position that is not too windswept. Such simple precautions will bring ample reward in a succession of gay colour throughout a long blooming period.

Any pot plant that is suitable for outdoor cultivation can bring colour and gaiety to the most dismal wall area, and flanking the front door bids a cheery welcome to callers. There is a wide selection of pot-holders ranging from the simplest wire ring to decorative wrought-iron designs, and hooks plugged firmly to the wall are all that is necessary to support any reasonable sized pot.

Numerous types of bulbs and plants will do well grown in this manner, and some of the most easily maintained include:

Flower	Colour	Blooming Period
Daffodils	Yellow	March to April
Hyacinths	White. Pinks. Blues	April to May

Flower	Colour	Blooming Period
Muscari	Blue	March to April
Tulips	Various	April to May
Lily of the valley	White	May
Asters	Various	June to Sept.
Antirrhinum	Various	June to Oct.
Begonia	Various	June to Oct.
Chrysanthemum	Various	Aug. to Nov.
Erica	Pink. Mauve. White	June to Nov.
Fuchsia	Red. Mauve	July to Oct.
Geranium	Reds. Pinks. White	June to Oct.
Marguerite	White	July to Sept.
Nasturtium	Various	June to Oct.
Nemesia	Various	June to Oct.
Salvias	Red	June to Oct.
Stocks	Various	April to July

Occasional feeding, regular watering and gentle forking of the top soil will reap dividends in a succession of blooms over a long period, and one of the advantages of 'pot gardening' is that ringing the changes is a two-minute task of simply changing the pots!

CLIMBERS

The finest disguise for an unsightly wall is one or more of the climbing plants which spill a profusion of blossom over the offending structure.

It is advisable to buy the climbers as young and sturdy pot plants and transfer them carefully to their allotted position, making sure that the roots and the base of the plants are at least nine inches away from the wall. Deep rich soil is desirable, and regular feeding and watering if the roots are housed in tubs or troughs.

Some climbers have their own devices for clinging to the wall, but when these are not present a simple trellis structure is useful. Otherwise the special wall pins or vine eyes which are obtainable from garden shops can be used.

Every climber has its own particular habit of growth and it is advisable to note this before attempting to train the shoots. A plant which is not allowed to follow its own special pattern of growth is never a success.

From a wide field of choice the following make an attractive show and are amiable plants under the hand of the novice.

Plant	Colour	Blooming Period
Clematis	Mauve. Pink. White	Spring and summer (likes its roots in shade and flowers in sun)
Cydonia japonica[1]	Red. Pink. White	Feb. to June (suitable for north walls)
Jasmine	White	Summer
Jasmine nudiflorum	Yellow	Winter (prefers a west wall)
Lapageria	Red. Pink. White	Summer (suitable for west walls)
Passion-flower	Red. White. Purple	Summer (south wall essential)

[1] Now often classified as *Chaenomeles lagenaria*, but still commonly known as cydonia, or Japanese flowering quince.

Plant	Colour	Blooming Period
Rose	Various	Summer
Wistaria	Mauve	May and June (prefers sheltered south aspect)

Where maximum coverage in the minimum time is required polygonum is the answer. The fastest grower of all climbers, polygonum will smother all before it in a mass of white flowering sprays. To keep it under control this rampant climber needs hard pruning after flowering in late autumn or early spring.

Among the annual climbers which can glorify a wall for a season are the morning glories (blue), convolvulus (pinks, reds, white), nasturtiums (gold, orange, red) and canary creeper (yellow), all of which may be raised from seed and produce an abundance of flowers throughout the summer months.

COURTYARDS

It takes little time or expense to transform the most un-promising backyard into a captivating courtyard with a show of flowers guaranteed to rouse the envy of those blessed with far greater opportunities.

If the yard is not already paved it is now possible to buy pastel-coloured paving stones as well as the usual off-white variety, and the laying of these is an easily accomplished task for the handyman. The high walls which usually surround the small yard take well to a thick coating of white or pale pink colour-wash, and provide a ready-made support for climbing plants, hanging pots and boxes. One of the advantages of flowers growing under these circumstances is that a continuous succession of blossom is achieved with the minimum of effort.

Having taken stock of the size of ground and wall area the first step is to plan positions of tubs and troughs to stand about the yard. All types of containers can be used, from old beer barrels to the 'ali-baba' crocks in which grandma kept her bread. Junk shops and scrap yards will often produce the most wonderful containers for a mere shilling or two, and it only remains to scrub them out and make drainage holes in the bottom before placing a thick layer of rough broken crock over the bottom and filling with soil. Wooden containers should be treated with Cuprinol before filling (see notes on window-boxes, page 127).

The next move should be to plan an attractive arrangement of hanging pots, wall boxes and climbing plants. A trellis fixed against the wall with a trough of soil at the base to hold the plant roots makes an ideal support for the type of climber which does not produce its own suckers with which to cling to the wall. Window type boxes can be fixed at suitable heights to the walls with angle brackets, and enough types of pot-plant holders are available to suit every conceivable taste.

Now comes the fun of choosing the plants for each container, and the choice is so wide that it is only possible here to mention some of those which will ensure a successful and attractive show even for the novice.

There are few plants that do not settle happily into a good-sized tub or trough, and anything that will grow in a window-box can be used in wall boxes. When wall boxes are to be used in the general scheme the tubs can be used to house flowering shrubs. Among the showy and easily cultivated ones are:

Shrub	Colour	Blooming Period
Camellia	White. Pink. Red	Blooming rather dependent upon the protection afforded. Prefers warm sheltered southern aspect to produce profuse early bloom.
Hydrangea	Pink. Blue. White	July to Sept.
Magnolia	White flushed pink	March to May. Large tub required. Does not like lime in the soil.
Rhododendron	White. Mauves. Pinks	May to June. Requires acid soil. Will not bloom in chalky soil.
Rose	All colours	Late spring to late autumn.

Tubs are also ideal for housing some of the bulbs and plants which are too large for window-boxes. The exquisite beauty and perfume of the various lilies need not be denied anyone who owns a tub, for they will bloom happily in a mixture of leaf-mould and sand, and should not be disturbed once they are planted until the tub becomes overcrowded. The pure white of Madonna lilies, the yellow, pink and purple of regal lilies, and the magnificent hues of the umbellatum varieties bring a touch of the exotic to the dullest corner.

Among the most interesting of the larger, taller plants suitable for tub gardening are:

Flower	Colour	Blooming Period
Chrysanthemum	Various	Aug. to Oct.
Columbine	Various	May to June
Dahlia	Various	July to Oct.
Delphinium	Pink. Blue. Mauve	July to Aug.
Foxglove	Pink. Mauve. White	July to Aug.
Hollyhock	Various	Aug. to Sept.
Kniphofia	Orange	Aug. to Sept.
Michaelmas daisy	Pinks. Mauves	Aug. to Oct.
Peony	Pink. Red. White	May to June
Phlox	Various	Aug. to Sept.

Last but by no means least of the happy tub dwellers is the water-lily, and while this flower is invariably associated with large pools and professional gardening, it will in fact bloom in serene beauty under the hand of the novice whose nearest approach to a lily pool is an old tub in a city yard. There are several exquisite varieties and any good garden specialist should be able to supply your choice.

Any receptacle about three feet deep which will hold water can be used. If circumstances permit the tub to be sunk up to its rim in the ground the effect is that of a miniature pool. About twelve inches of heavy loam should be placed in the bottom of the tub before adding about eighteen inches of water.

The only essential points to remember are that two or three oxygenating plants *must* be planted along with the lily. These plants will take a few days to settle in, and during this period the water will turn brown or green. *On no account* should the water be drained off. As soon as the oxygenating plants have established themselves they will commence to do their work of keeping the water fresh and clean.

Two good oxygenating plants are *Elodea canadensis* and *Callitriche autumnalis*, and two of either would be sufficient for a tub housing one lily plant. A worth-while addition to the tub would be two or three 'ramshorn' snails, who can be relied upon to do any necessary scavenging!

If space allows for a larger tub or tank, the lilies may be joined by other water plants such as the water iris, marsh marigold or flowering rush. For the true flower-lover there is no limit to what can be achieved with the minimum outlay and the most restricted opportunities.

BUDDLEIAS AND BUTTERFLIES

Do you like butterflies? All the exotic rainbow-coloured ones I mean.

And do you like lounging in the sun in a quiet garden?

You do? Then plant a buddleia in a sunny position and when the long graceful flower sprays are in bloom take a chair and sit close to the bush.

The scent of the flowers and the soft fluttering of exquisitely tinted wings are a wonderful antidote to the speed of modern living. And while ever you have a buddleia you will never be short of butterflies.

Kill or Cure

The modern chemist's shop with its neat packages gives no hint that many of the 'modern' drugs are in fact the very ones that were once used in an aura of magic mixed with astrology, and among them the narcotics have a rather special place.

The beautiful deadly nightshade with its vivid purple flowers and glossy black berries contains a deadly poison. It is said that an Italian used it to poison beautiful women and from his gruesome activities sprang the name of belladonna. Today it has a valuable place in eye surgery and is used internally for several complaints.

The mandrake may have been the original anaesthetic, the root being steeped in wine and a drink given to the patient before treatment. This 'death wine' is said to have been given by the women of Roman times to prisoners being crucified, and it is widely believed that this was the wine offered on the sponge to Jesus during His crucifixion. In the late nineteenth century an alkaloid called hyoscine was isolated from the mandrake and found to produce insensibility to pain. Even greater sources of hyoscine have since been found in the thorn apple, which for centuries has been associated with the Devil and evil spirits. A large, showy, highly poisonous and evil-smelling plant, it is also used in some types of herbal cigarettes for the alleviation of asthma.

Another unpleasantly scented and very poisonous plant is the henbane, from which the drug known as 'twilight sleep' was obtained. It has long been used as a general pain-killer and once found popularity as a cure for toothache.

Many do not realize that while the smoking or chewing of the narcotic produced from the milky juice of the opium poppy can reduce a human being to the borders of insanity, the seeds are quite harmless and are widely used in confectionery and as a garnish for various continental breads. The gloomy-looking monkshood, which today provides a useful drug, is so poisonous that even animals are careful to avoid it, and in the days when wolves roamed these islands it was used to bait their traps.

Our wild hemlock, once the favourite potion for poisoning king and commoner alike, and the reputed liquidator of Socrates in 399 B.C., is nevertheless a valuable sedative and narcotic. The Romans used it mixed with opium as an execution drug, and the Greeks found it useful in disposing of their enemies. As this is a common plant, and one very like other harmless ones of its family, care should be taken by flower-lovers to distinguish it from its cousins.

An attractive plant whose beautiful scarlet berries are a great temptation to children is the white bryony, but as every part of the plant is highly poisonous—often fatally— its dangers should be instilled into any child living in or visiting the countryside. A member of the cucumber family, it adorns our hedgerows in wild abandon, and when properly used is a valuable aid in the treatment of gout, rheumatism and some bronchial troubles.

These and many others are the stuff from which medicines are made. In the glowing petal of a flower, in the juice of a glossy berry, lies the power for good or evil. If their names appear on the chemist's package, all is well. If you meet them in the hedgerow, admire them—but leave them where they are!

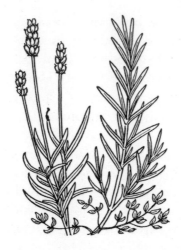

CHAPTER 16

The Herb Garden

He who cultivates a herb garden enjoys the fun of forging a direct link with his Elizabethan ancestors, but although the Elizabethans were perhaps the greatest of the herb gardeners they were by no means the first to cultivate plants for practical use. The early monasteries were seats of medicine as well as scholarship, and even today around the sites of medieval monasteries prolific crops of herbs, particularly the narcotics and pain-killers, still bear silent witness to the monastic growers who toiled to bring relief and recovery to the sick and ailing of their day, and many of the herbs grown at that time are still widely used in modern medicine.

Several of our best-known herbs were actually introduced into Britain by the Romans, who imported from the Mediterranean shores such plants as celandine, rosemary, southernwood, sage, thyme and many others, and it was that famous physician Dioscorides who compiled the *materia medica* that were to become the basis of herbal medicine for sixteen centuries.

The only real difference between the herb gardens of today
and yesterday is that whereas we can select our plants purely
for pleasure the choice of past generations was influenced
largely by necessity. The most important inhabitants of
early gardens were those cultivated for the express purpose of
coping with the disease and evil smells of an insanitary age.
House floors were strewn with sweet-smelling herbs, and in
the courtrooms rue and other disinfectant herbs were used to
cut down the risk of infection from plague and other diseases
that beset the people who were brought to trial from the
filthy disease-ridden confines of the prisons; and as extra protection the judges always carried posies of antiseptic herbs.
Narcotics were cultivated for pain-killing purposes, and a
wide variety of plants were used in the treatment of both
physical and mental ailments.

To these essential plants the ladies of the Tudor period
added the herbs that provided them with perfumes, cosmetics,
tisanes and sweetmeats, and every house of any standing
boasted a large herb garden that was the especial responsibility
of the lady and her maids. Indeed, it is to them that we owe
our gratitude for many of the flowers and fruits that we take
for granted today, for it was from their gardens that rasp-
berries, strawberries and several tree fruits, as well as lavender,
rosemary and many other sweetly scented flowers, really
developed.

It is not absolutely essential for us to use plants for either
medical or culinary purposes, and the attractive appearance
of a herb garden is alone sufficient to make its cultivation
worth while, but it is infinitely more pleasurable – and profit-
able – if we do use the plants we grow. The actual preparation and cultivation are very simple and this type of garden
has the advantage of being easily run and highly adaptable to

every shape and size of plot. Most plants will thrive in a medium light soil, preferably with a sunny south-west aspect, and with a sheltering wall or fence behind. Failing such a shelter, a good wind and frost break can be provided by a shrubby background of evergreens.

A wall or fence is the ideal support for a selection of old-fashioned roses (for use in rose petal conserve, pot-pourri, etc.) and jasmine (for flower waters and oils). If such a support is not available the climbers can be trained to scramble up rustic poles or trellis.

The design of any herb garden, large or small, is entirely a matter of taste, but it is well to remember one or two important points. First, there must be plenty of walking space among the plants. Paths of crazy paving or flagstones are ideal, but provided they are kept closely clipped camomile and thyme make delightful paths, giving up their delicious perfume as they are walked upon.

Provided the plot is large enough a sundial, birdbath or garden seat will bring added charm to the garden. The plans on page 149 will give a guide to the beginner, and can be used as basic ideas on which to plan an individual garden.

Before laying out the plot it should be well dug and some good compost or manure worked in if the soil is very poor or lacking in body, and a fine tilth obtained prior to the introduction of the plants. Never over-stock the beds to start with as the plants will quickly spread. It is usually better to obtain young plants from a good nurseryman or cuttings or divisions from anyone who is already growing herbs. Most good seed catalogues list a range of herbs, but to start an entire garden from seed is liable to be a long and tedious business.

There are so many interesting plants from which to select

PLATE XII Indoor Plants (*See key overleaf*)

(*facing p. 144*)

Primula

Cyclamen   Thorn   Geranium

that the gardener who has never before explored this territory is often at a loss to know which to choose. Much depends on whether the garden is to be purely ornamental or whether it is intended to serve some practical use as well. The cook who likes to provide dishes with a subtle flavour will undoubtedly wish to introduce some of the culinary herbs which can do so much towards turning a perfectly ordinary set of ingredients into a gourmet's delight. Another person may prefer to grow the herbs which for generations have been used by country folk and chemist alike for the relief of such ailments as coughs, colds and digestive troubles. Yet another person may be interested in the cosmetic and perfume plants, while someone else may wish only to sit on a garden bench in the perfumed peace of a beautiful garden with the awesome reflection that herbs have clothed the earth since the third day of Creation. At all events, there is something for everyone in the vast company of plants, and the following short list may help a little in the choice.

❋   ❋   ❋

Angelica. Large showy plant. Used for coughs and bronchial ailments, also the stems are candied as a sweetmeat.

Bergamot. Beautiful sweetly perfumed plant. Likes deep moist soil. Contains antiseptic oils.

Broom. Bright showy plant. Used in kidney, liver and heart diseases.

Camomile. Sweetly perfumed. Makes beautiful lawns and paths and resists drought. Used in British pharmacopoeia as tonic and sedative. Makes excellent hair rinse for blondes.

K

Caraway. Used in digestive troubles. Seeds used in cakes and bread.

Chervil. Dainty plant with anise flavour. Used to be eaten at Easter time. Improves salads and soups.

Chives. Grass-like. Mild onion flavour. Used in salads, soups and with cheese.

Coltsfoot. Bright yellow flowers before the leaves. Used for asthmatic and bronchial troubles, also coltsfoot rock sweetmeat.

Coriander. Mentioned in the Bible. Stimulant. Seeds used to flavour confectionery and liqueurs. An ingredient of cake spice.

Dill. Sharp, aromatic flavour. Used in pickling. Adds interest to *canapé* spreads, egg and cheese dishes, meat and poultry.

Elecampane. Beautiful plant used by Elizabethans as a candied sweetmeat. Now used in bronchial and kidney troubles.

Fennel. Mentioned in Anglo-Saxon herbals. Known as the 'fish herb' but also useful in meat, egg, cheese and salad dishes.

Florentine Iris. Exquisite plant often called the fleur-de-lis. Its violet-scented root (orris root) is used in perfume and toilet preparations.

Foxgloves. Attractive showy plant, providing digitalis used in heart complaints.

Hyssop. Beautiful plant, evergreen. Used in bronchial ailments. Oil distilled from leaves gives fragrance to some liqueurs and perfumes.

Lavender. Sweet perfume, attractive flowers that keep their fragrance long after drying.

Lemon Balm. Lemony-mint flavour used in perfumes and cooking. Add to fruits, jellies and wine cups.

Lemon Verbena. Leaves useful in pot-pourri and perfume bags.

Lily of the Valley. Exquisite perfume. Drug obtained from it considered safer for heart ailments than that obtained from foxgloves. Appears in many paintings of the Virgin Mary.

Marigold. Bright and cheerful addition to the garden. Its petals bring colour and flavour to soups and stews. Stimulant.

Marjoram. Pungent oil used in perfumery. Used as savoury herb.

Marshmallow. Attractive plant with large pale pink flowers. Used in the relief of all inflammatory conditions.

Mint. Fragrant digestive herb. Used with savoury jelly, lamb, soups and sweetmeats, also in mint tea.

Mullein. Grown by early monasteries in their physic gardens. Used now in soothing ointments and for chest complaints.

Periwinkle. Pretty evergreen plant. Tonic. Makes a good ointment for inflammatory conditions.

Poppy. Colourful addition to the garden, used by country folk for toothache and nerve pains.

Rose. Beautiful, sweetly perfumed. For confectionery and perfume.

Rue. Old disinfectant herb. Now known to be source of valuable drug for treatment of weakened blood-vessels and high-blood-pressure conditions.

Saffron Crocus. Gave its name to Saffron Walden. Used for dyeing ruffs in bygone days. Stamens used to colour and flavour saffron cake.

St. John's Wort. Pretty, antiseptic, astringent. Used in chest complaints.

Salad Burnet. Dainty plant, taken by Pilgrim Fathers to the

New World. Fragrant, tonic. Used in salads and sauces and in wine cups.

Savory. Very valuable for all savoury dishes and stuffings.

Southernwood. Dainty, feathery-leaved plant with attractive, pungent fragrance. Tonic, antiseptic. Deters moths.

Sweet Cicely. Tall, beautiful, sweet-scented. Gives its fragrance to chartreuse. Sometimes used in place of incense. Use in salads, soups, dressings and herb butters.

Tansy. Attractive plant. Tonic. Used in tansy cake and pudding eaten at Easter.

Tarragon. Almost indispensable to the gourmet. Used carefully in sauces, vegetable dishes, with mushrooms, vinegars and butters.

Thyme. Fragrant. Used sparingly in all savoury dishes. Makes springy and beautiful garden paths and lawns.

Violet. Pretty, fragrant, antiseptic. Excellent for sore throats. Used in perfume and candied as sweetmeats.

White Horehound. Used constantly since 450 B.C. Beautiful plant, used in bronchial and digestive ailments. Pleasant flavour makes it attractive to children.

NOTE. See Chapter 9 for method of drying plants for storage. Roots and thick stems will take a little longer than flowers and leaves.

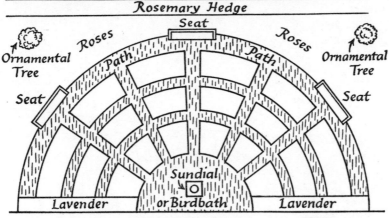

Support with Climbing Roses & Jasmine

Rosemary Hedge

Seat

Roses   Path   Path   Roses

Ornamental Tree   Ornamental Tree

Seat   Seat

Sundial

or Birdbath

Lavender   Lavender

Garden Seats banked around with Lavender
Crazy Paving Paths with Thyme between spaces } ☐ Herb Beds } KEY

(*a*) Especially suited to a large plot.

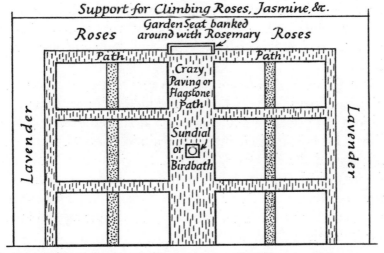

Support for Climbing Roses, Jasmine, &c.

Roses   Garden Seat banked around with Rosemary   Roses

Path   Path

Lavender   Crazy Paving or Flagstone Path   Lavender

Sundial or Birdbath

KEY:- ▦ Camomile or Thyme Paths   ☐ Beds of Chosen Herbs

(*b*) Readily adaptable to all sizes of plot.

PLANS FOR A HERB GARDEN

CHAPTER 17

Gardener's Corner

The dedicated gardener knows all the answers. His bookshelves are lined with volumes covering the subject from every possible angle. He knows exactly what to do and when to do it, and will prophesy what will happen long before the event.

But for every gardener of this calibre there are hundreds who have neither the time nor the inclination to master the subject, and while they earnestly desire a lovely garden filled with flowers their thirst for technical knowledge hovers only round the fringes. What plants will make a colourful border, which flowers will produce the strongest scent, and how to smother the weeds are the points which interest them most, and the following charts give the simple answers to all three questions.

The flowers listed for scent by no means include *all* perfumed flowers, but cover those which have particularly strong or sweet scent. A selection of these planted about the garden will shed their fragrance over the entire area, and perfume from beds planted close to doorways and beneath windows will pervade the whole house.

To those who love flowers but loathe weeding the plants named in the first list can be recommended. Colourful and vigorous, they can be relied upon to run riot and smother every weed in their path. A watchful eye should be kept on some of these boisterous members of the flower world lest in their exuberance they smother not only weeds but other garden favourites!

Listed under their separate colours are a selection of plants which can be relied upon to make a showy garden, and any good nurseryman will supply the plants of your choice.

✳   ✳   ✳

PLANTS FOR CLOSE COVERAGE

Alchemilla vulgaris	Lamium maculatum
Arabis	Lanata
Aubrietia	Lysimachia nummularia
Campanula	Polygonum campanulatum
Cerastium	Pulmonaria
Cornus canadensis	Saxifrage
Cotoneaster horizontalis	Sedum
Cotoneaster salicifolia Herbst	Stachys grandiflora
fleur	Thrift
Dianthus	Thyme
Helianthemum	Vinca minor
Hypericum	

PLANTING FOR FRAGRANCE

PLANTS

Alyssum, sweet   Pinks
Dianthus   Scabious, annual
Heliotrope   Ten-week (and other) stocks
Lily of the valley   Tobacco (Nicotiana)
Mignonette   Wallflowers
Night-scented stock

SHRUBS

Choisya   Lavender   Syringa
Jasmine   Roses   Viburnum carlesii

NOTE. Rose perfume varies considerably from one variety to another, and a visit to a rose-grower when the flowers are in bloom is the best method of selecting the varieties with the most appealing scent to individual taste.

❊   ❊   ❊

SOME PLANTS WITH WHITE OR CREAM FLOWERS

Aquilegia   Galega   Papaver
Arabis   Gladiolus   Penstemon
Aster   Gypsophila   Phlox
Astilbe   Helleborus   Pyrethrum
Bellis   Iberis   Sidalcea
Campanula   Iris   Thalictrum
Chrysanthemum   Lavatera   Veronica
Dianthus   Lilium   Viola

SOME PLANTS WITH YELLOW, GOLD OR BRONZE FLOWERS

Achillea	Gaillardia	Montbretia
Alyssum	Geum	Physalis
Aquilegia	Helenium	Rudbeckia
Calceolaria	Helianthus	Solidago
Chrysanthemum	Iris	Trollius
Coreopsis	Lupinus	Verbascum
Doronicum	Mimulus	Viola

SOME PLANTS WITH PINK FLOWERS

Aster	Geranium	Papaver
Aubrietia	Gladiolus	Penstemon
Campanula	Gypsophila	Phlox
Chrysanthemum	Lupinus	Saxifrage
Delphinium	Paeonia	Sedum
Dianthus		

SOME PLANTS WITH MAUVE FLOWERS

Anemone	Digitalis	Lupinus
Aster	Erigeron	Nepeta
Aubrietia	Iris	Stachys
Campanula	Lavender	Thalictrum

SOME PLANTS WITH BLUE FLOWERS

Aconitum	Campanula	Lupinus
Ajuga	Centaurea	Nepeta
Anchusa	Delphinium	Polemonium
Aquilegia	Echinops	Pulmonaria
Aster	Iris	Veronica
Calanche	Linum	Viola

SOME PLANTS WITH RED FLOWERS

Achillea	Dianthus	Paeonia
Adonis	Gaillardia	Papaver
Alstromeria	Geranium	Penstemon
Aquilegia	Geum	Phlox
Aster	Gladiolus	Potentilla
Bellis	Kniphofia	Pyrethrum
Centranthus	Lobelia	Salvia
Chrysanthemum	Lychnis	Spiraea

Calendar of Floral Decoration

	Flowers	Trees and Shrubs	Coloured Bark	Foliage	Berries, Seed-heads, etc.

JANUARY	Anemones
	Daffodils
	Helleborus
	  niger
	Freesias
	Mimosa
	Narcissus
	Snowdrops
	Violets
		Chimonanthus
		  fragrans
		Erica
		Garrya catkins
		Hamamelis
		Jasmine
		Laurestinus
		Lonicera
		Viburnum
		  fragrans
			Berberis
			Cornus
			Kerria
			Pinus
			Salix
			Sorbus
				Euonymus
				Veronica
				Rhododendron
				Berberis
				Lonicera
				Rosemary
				Hothouse ferns
					Euonymus
					Cotoneaster
					Pyracantha
					Ornamental
					  gourds
					Dried grasses

FEBRUARY	Aconites
	Daffodils
	Freesias
	Helleborus
	  niger
	Muscari
	Snowdrops
		Erica
		Garrya catkins
		Chimonanthus
		  fragrans
		Daphne
		  mezereum
		Hamamelis
		Jasmine
		Viburnum
		  fragrans
			Berberis
			Cornus
			Kerria
			Pinus
			Salix
			Sorbus
				Box
				Cyclamen
				Berberis
				Laurel
				Rosemary
				Hothouse ferns
					Cotoneaster
					Pyracantha
					Gourds
					Dried flowers
					Dried grasses

	Flowers	Trees and Shrubs	Coloured Bark	Foliage	Berries, Seed-heads, etc.
MARCH	Daffodils Doronicum Anemone Armeria Polyanthus Primroses Muscari Violets	Almond Berberis Forsythia Kerria Daphne mezereum Magnolia	Berberis Cornus Kerria Pinus Salix Sorbus	Berberis Box Fir Palm Self-foliage Young leaves	

APRIL	Armeria
	Bellis
	Daffodils
	Narcissus
	Primula
	  auricula
	Polyanthus
	Primroses
	Violets
	Tulips
		Almond
		Cherry
		Forsythia
		Kerria
		  japonica
		Ribes
		Magnolia
			Pinus
			Cornus
			Salix
				Self-foliage
				Young leaves
				Evergreens	

	Flowers	Trees and Shrubs	Coloured Bark	Foliage	Berries, Seed-heads, etc.
MAY	Achillea Aquilegia Calendulas Dicentra Eremerus Geum Incarvillea Iris Lily of the valley Pyrethrum Ranunculus Wallflowers	Broom Cherry Chestnut Cornus kousa Hawthorn Lilac Weigelia	Silver birch	Beech Larch Silver birch Willow Young ferns Self-foliage	
JUNE	Anchusa Campanula Coreopsis Delphinium Erigeron Foxgloves Iceland poppies Marguerites Peonies Lupins Pinks Scabiosa Sweet peas Penstemons	Azalea Buddleia Deutzia Lilac Lonicera Philadelphus Spiraea Rhododendron Weigelia		Beech Elm Lime Birch Self-foliage Willow	

	Flowers	Trees and Shrubs	Coloured Bark	Foliage	Berries, Seed-heads, etc.
JULY	Astilbe	Buddleia	Pinus	Beech	
	Antirrhinums	Deutzia		Bracken	
	Carnations	Hydrangea		Ivy	
	Cornflowers	Hypericum		Silver birch	
	Catananche	Spiraea		Privet	
	Godetia	Jasmine		Rosemary	
	Helianthus	Lavender		Willow	
	Lychnis	Philadelphus			
	Nepeta	Laburnum			
	Nigella				
	Roses				
	Stocks				
AUGUST	Alstromeria	Escallonia	Pinus	Birch	Gourds
	Asters	Hydrangea		Bracken	Oats
	Dahlias	Hops		Ferns	Wheat
	Gaillardia	Hypericum		Larch	Barley
	Gladiolus	Lavender		Ivy	Sloes
	Hollyhocks	Potentilla		Maple	Wild arum
	Larkspur	Tamarisk		Self-foliage	
	Nasturtium				
	Marguerites				
	Gypsophila				
	Solidago				
	Clarkia				

	Flowers	Trees and Shrubs	Coloured Bark	Foliage	Berries, Seed-heads, etc.
SEPTEMBER	Asters Helenium Helianthus Galega Gladiolus Cornflowers Kniphofia Montbretia Phlox Rudbeckia Gaillardia Salvia Statice Heliopsis	Hypericum Hydrangea Buddleia Perowskia Tamarisk Veronica		Maple Silver fir Berberis Golden privet Beech Ivy Virginia creeper Ferns Evergreens	Clematis Dried hops Grapes Physalis Pyracantha Rowan Cotoneaster
OCTOBER	Anemones Asters Cornflowers Cosmea Chrysanthemum Gaillardia Rudbeckia Helichrysum Helianthus Kniphofia Michaelmas daisies Solidago	Fuchsia Jasmine	Cornus Willow	Beech Bracken Maple Virginia creeper Autumn leaves Ivy	Bryony Hips Haws Clematis Cotoneaster Euonymus Pyracantha Physalis Ribes

	Flowers	Trees and Shrubs	Coloured Bark	Foliage	Berries, Seed-heads, etc.
NOVEMBER	Anemones Armeria Chrysanthemum Helleborus niger Iris Chrysanthemum koreanum Freesias Violets	Jasmine Lonicera	Berberis Cornus Kerria Salix Perowskia Sorbus	Berberis Cyclamen Dianthus Evergreens Hothouse ferns Preserved leaves	Hips Haws Physalis Bryony Euonymus Pyracantha Dried seed-heads Snowberries
DECEMBER	Anemones Helleborus niger Chrysanthemum Freesias Mimosa Carnations Violets Statice Forced bulbs	Chimonanthus fragrans Erica Azalea Jasmine Viburnum fragrans	Berberis Cornus Kerria Salix Perowskia Sorbus Pinus	Cyclamen Evergreens Preserved leaves Ivy Hothouse ferns	Holly Mistletoe Physalis Dried flowers Dried seed-heads Cotoneaster Dried grasses Snowberries